The

Story

of

Dunsany

Castle

Published by: Carty/Lynch, Dunsany, Co. Meath, Ireland
                  July 2000

Layout: A. & J. Print Dunshaughlin Ltd.
Cover Design: Don Harper, Artwerk, 145 Pearse Street,
                  Dublin 2, Ireland

© Carty/Lynch 2000
ISBN 0 9517382 1 6

Printed in Ireland by:
Colour Books Ltd., Baldoyle, Dublin 13, Ireland.

WRITTEN & COMPILED

BY

MALACHY LYNCH & MARY-ROSE CARTY

INCORPORATING

NOTES & INFORMATION COLLECTED

BY

THE LATE DAVID W. LYNCH

(Photograph: Paul Tierney)   *Dunsany Castle (Southwest Wing)*

INTRODUCTION BY EDWARD PLUNKETT, LORD DUNSANY

Home Archaeology

My grandfather used to say the Plunketts were an old family, who bought their books and furniture new. He could have added that Plunketts never throw anything out.

The walls are alive with portraits of dead Dunsany Plunketts. They speak through their letters and diaries; they speak through their love of art and architecture. The house begs a silent dialogue of past and present. It's a work in progress, like this study.

July, 2000

CONTENTS

Page No.

Aerial Photograph of Dunsany Castle

Dunsany Castle flanked by the Twin Dunes

(Photograph: Paul Tierney)

Dunsany

The Twin dunes stand before it and beneath
Their tree and dark summits the Skane river flows
An old, divine Earth emanation glows.

About it though no longer battles breathe
For time puts all men's swords in his red sheathe:
And gentler now the air from Tara blows
Thus in the royallest ground that Ireland knows
Stands your sheer house in immemorial Meath.

It stands for actions done and days endured.
Old causes that God, guiding time, espoused
Who does not brook the undeserving long.
I found there pleasant chambers filled with song.
(And never were the muses better housed -
Repose and dignity and fame assured).

Oliver St John Gogarty

© Lord Dunsany

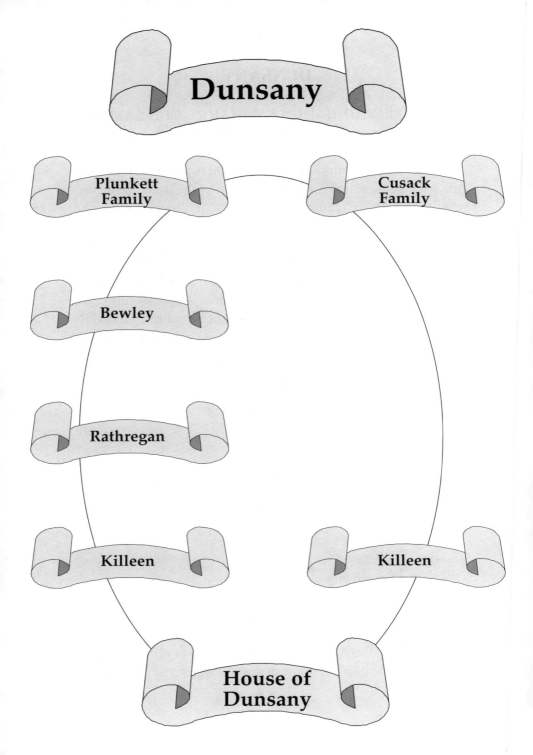

Dunsany

Plunkett Family

Cusack Family

Bewley

Rathregan

Killeen

Killeen

House of Dunsany

DUNSANY

DUN SAMHNAIDH - DUN SAMHAIGE - DUN SAMAIG -
historians vary in the Irish form and in tracing the derivation
of the name. Many favour the theory that it is the fort of a
chieftain named Samna or Samhain, others that it derives from
the ancient autumnal three-day festival of the dead. However,
there is a local tradition that links it closely with the
neighbouring royal Hill of Tara at the height of its glory. The
Gaelic kings and chieftains of old regarded war as a seasonal
occupation - the "open season" being from 17th March to 29th
September. In any event this too seems to have been common
practise with Roman armies of conquest who also retired to
winter quarters. Tradition has it that the armies of the Ard Ri
of Tara followed this practice and retired to the neighbouring
lowlands in the fall each year and hence the name Dun Samhna
(Fort of Autumn).

It is recorded that during this period there was a settlement in
Dun Samhna of the dynastic family of Ua Cellaig, one of the
four tribes of Tara, consisting of betaghs and retainers in
addition to numerous men, women and children who claimed
to be the "family" of the resident chief, who indeed had not
only a wife but a large number of concubines as well. This
was long before the arrival of Hugh de Lacy as Lord of Meath.
Hugh de Lacy granted the barony of Skryne to Adam de Feipo,
and de Feipo granted Killeen to his relative Geoffrey de Cusack
'to be held by suit and service of the titular Barons of Skryne'.

Killeen is an oddly shaped tract of land, roughly rectangular,
with the wedge-shaped parish of Dunsany penetrating far into
the rectangle. The popular theory is that it was occupied by an
Irish chieftain and his retainers, who remained ensconced, there

wedded to their Celtic way of life, while Norman "improvements" were imposed all around them.

Dunsany does not feature in any twelfth or thirteenth-century charters and the first mention we have of the parish is in the ecclesiastical taxation lists of 1305. The church did not form any part of Adam de Feipo's early grants and was never subject to Saint Mary's Abbey, Dublin.

However, we are concerned with the story of the castle built here about 1181 and more particularly with the life and times, the fortunes and misfortunes, of its occupants.

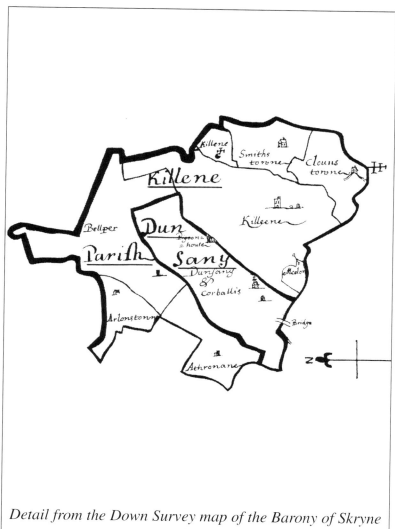

Detail from the Down Survey map of the Barony of Skryne
(1657)

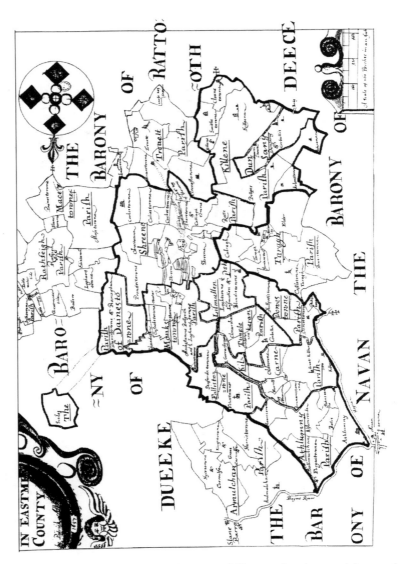

The Down Survey map of the barony of Skryne showing parishes and townlands. Black outline shows lands granted to Adam de Feypo. (Photographed from the original in the Bibliotheque Nationale, Paris and published by the Ordnance Survey Office, Southampton, in 1908.)

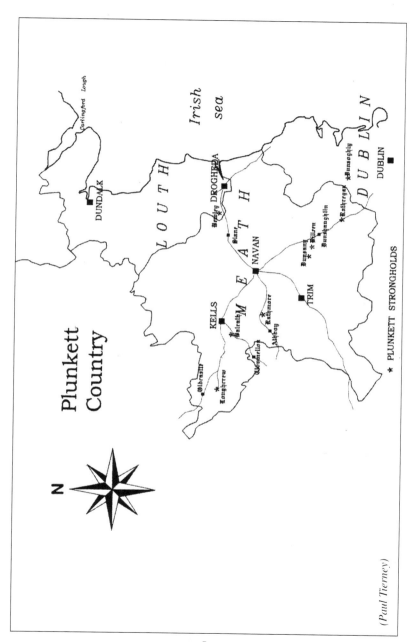

Plunkett
Country

N

Irish sea

Darlingford Lough

L O U T H

DUNDALK

DROGHEDA
Medley

M E A T H

Slane
NAVAN

KELLS

Balrath
Girley
Ulcymullon

Rathmarr
Rathmore
Althboy

TRIM

Olbrastle

Longtrrw

Burgsart
Kilurn
Dunshanghlin

Rathrrge
*Dunsoghly

D U B L I N

DUBLIN

* PLUNKETT STRONGHOLDS

(Paul Tierney)

THE PLUNKETTS

When and how this family first arrived in Ireland is still a matter of conjecture. There isn't any conflict regarding the fact that they settled originally in Bewley (or Beaulieu) in Co. Louth. What is in question, however, is the date of their arrival and their nationality: whether in fact they were Danes who settled in that area in the last quarter of the eleventh century or earlier, or whether they were Normans and had formed part of de Lacy's retinue at the time of the Norman conquest.

Many historical sources favour the Danish origin thesis, notably the Carew Manuscripts on the Temporal Nobility (Book of Howth) which states, "this family came in with the Danes, thereof they still have, as yet special monuments". Tantalisingly, the manuscript does not expand on the "special monuments" but one wonders if the instruction in the will of the first Lord of Dunsany, Christopher (dated 1st August, 1461) - "Item, I will, the old hanging of green and white bide in the hall at Donsany" - could be one such monument. Again, William Lynch in 1830, in his own definitive work on the feudal baronies established in Ireland during the reign of Henry II states: "It is generally reported that the family of Plunkett was settled in Ireland anterior to the arrival of Henry II, and though there are reasons for believing this tradition to be true, yet it cannot be supported by authentic evidence." Henry II reigned from 1154 to 1189. Lynch then goes on to state that it is recorded that in the reign of Henry III (1216 -1272) "and how long before has not been ascertained" that "Walter Plunkett was seised of the estate of CLUINAGHLYS in fee", and his grandson, John, who was "possessed of the lordship of Bewley", founded a church within his manor. In the 1789 revision of Lodge's Peerage, it is stated that there were

Plunketts in Bewley in the last quarter of the eleventh century, and that John Plunkett died in 1082 and his son (named either William or Walter) died in 1088. However, these dates cannot be authenticated nor indeed is there any continuity in the family tree to John who built the church at Bewley. Debrett too is of the opinion that "this noble family is of Danish origin but its settlement in Ireland is so remote that nothing can be ascertained as to the precise period."

Edward McLysaght in his work on the origin of Irish families has, however, no difficulty in stating categorically that the name Plunkett is a corruption of "blanchet" derived from blanc (white) and is of French, not Danish origin, introduced to Ireland at the time of the Norman Invasion. This is corroborated in Seventy Years Young: Memories of Elizabeth, Countess of Fingall, which indicates that the family tree traces the Plunketts to Allaine, a descendant of the first Duke of Normandy who headed a troop of horsemen at the battle of Hastings.

Family tradition in Dunsany, passed down by word of mouth, is that they are of Danish origin and, when the Normans invaded Ireland, the Plunketts did not oppose them but subsequently married them and became their bishops and lawyers and, later, their barons. Whatever the Plunkett origin may have been - Danish or Norman - it may fairly be said that it is one of the most distinguished names in the history of this country.

Through marriage, the family expanded into Meath from Bewley in Louth. First to Rathregan and then to Killeen, Dunsany, Rathmore, Balrath and also Dunsoghly, near St. Margaret's, Co. Dublin.

Many important historical papers belonging to the Dunsany Plunkett family were lost when the Bermingham Tower, Dublin Castle, was burnt down in 1684, as this had been used as a state record repository. Fire again destroyed many important family documents in January 1923, when Horace Plunkett's home in Kilteragh, Co. Dublin, was mined and then burnt. Horace had been sifting through family documents whilst preparing to write his memoirs.

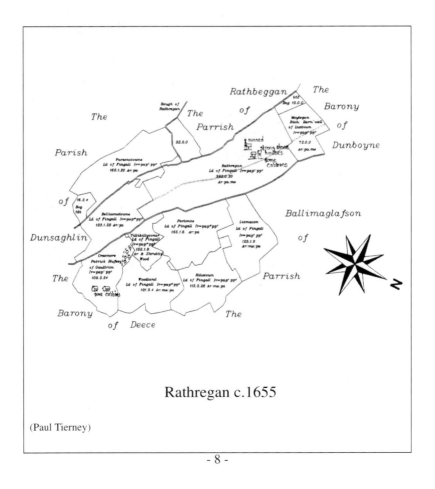

Rathregan c.1655

(Paul Tierney)

RATHREGAN

Rathregan lies south of Dunshaughlin, Co. Meath, close to Batterstown.[1] Richard Plunkett, brother of John, Lord of Beaulieu, inherited Rathregan. He is mentioned in a writ dated 1310, along with the Meath families of Le Tuite and Cusack. The Plunketts resided in Rathregan until 1402 when Christopher Plunkett married Joan de Cusack, heiress of Killeen Castle, and subsequently moved his residence there.

Sir Christopher Plunkett, (Lord of Killeen, Feudal Baron of Rathregan, Sheriff of Meath, Deputy Governor of Ireland to Sir Thomas Stanley and subsequently, to Richard, Duke of York) and Lady Joan had seven sons and three daughters. The eldest, John, was heir to Killeen; Christopher founded the Plunkett House of Dunsany, Co. Meath; Thomas founded the Plunkett House of Rathmore, Co. Meath (between Navan and Athboy); Robert founded the Plunkett House of Dunsoghly, Co. Dublin (St. Margaret's); Richard died without family; Edward founded the Plunkett House of Balrath, Co. Meath (between Clonmellon and Kells); and Edmund became a priest.

Rathregan remained in the possession of the Plunkett family and, in the Down Survey of 1655, the map of the Parish of Rathregan shows Lord Fingall (Papist) as the proprietor of 382 acres lands profitable and 33 acres unprofitable "bogg"; the accompanying notes refer to Rathregan as containing an old ruined church, a strong stone house in repair and some cabins. Now only undulations indicate where the castle stood; any imposing residence has long since been eradicated from the landscape.

[1] William Lynch has handed down the most explicit information on the initial estate of the Plunkett family in Meath.

"Richard Plunket, brother of John, Lord of Beaulieu, besides a considerable paternal estate, made large acquirements by his connexion with the families of Blundus, or Le Blunt, Lord of Rathregan, (who was summoned by writ to the Parliament of 1310), Le Tuite and Cusack. His son and heir, Richard, called Richard Plunket Junior, was Lord of Rathregan, Tullaghanogue, and Killallon; and on the 14th of March 1358, by a deed in the French language, Lionel the King's son, by the title of 'Lionell Fitz, a noble Roi Dengleterre & de Fraunce, Comit D'Ulnestre & Seigneur de Connaught,' appointed his dear and well beloved Roger de Heygham and Richard Plunket his Attornies General, to do and answer in all things for him in Ireland, and to hold his courts by themselves or their deputies in his Barony of Ratowth and seigniory of Coly, etc. This appointment, which was, according to the practice of that day, a sort of deputation of power to represent the prince who gave it, rendered Richard Plunket one of the most influential lords within the Pale, by placing under his authority the provinces of Ulster and of Connaught, which were then separate jurisdictions, exclusively belonging to Lionel, Duke of Clarence. There are various entries to be found by which it appears that Lord Richard's possessions were extremely extensive; and by the settlement of the Loughgower, Moreton, Dunshaughlin, and other estates belonging to the family of Berford, his sons were made remainder men in tail male to those estates.

"When a Parliament was summoned in the year 1374, a writ was issued to him, as well as to Walter Cusack, Baron of Killeen, amongst the other Earls, Magnates, and Proceres of Ireland; and on that occasion, it should be observed, his kinsman Richard Plunket, already mentioned, was summoned amongst the Lords assistant or Members of the King's Privy Council. He died soon after this Parliament; and it appears by certain entails that he had two sons, John and Christopher; the former of whom must have died without issue, as his name occurs not after that period.

"Christopher was a minor at his father's death; and it was not until 1391 that he was sued to take on him the order of knighthood, according to law; for which purpose he was found by inquisition to possess the necessary qualifications in the county of Meath alone. At this time the title of the family, we should conclude, was Baron of Rathregan, as it was there Lord Richard and his son resided; and the castle of Rathregan, as the place of residence, must be considered to have been the 'caput barony'; but soon after, Sir Christopher Plunket married Johanna the daughter and heiress of Sir Lucas Cusack, Baron of Killeen, the son and heir of Sir Walter Cusack, Chevalier, who was summoned by writ to several parliaments, and particularly to that of the 48th of Edward the Third, to which Richard Plunket was summoned at the same time. By this marriage Sir Christopher acquired, in right of his wife, Lady Johanna, the lordships and manors of Killeen, Kilskire, Killallon,

Clonmacduffe, and Clony, with advowsons of the churches lying within the same. This marriage took place in or before the year 1402, while parliamentary dignities, as declared in the 51st. Edw.III., were enjoyed by tenure, as on the 3rd May in the former year, Sir Christopher and his wife were ordered to be released from the debt of £300, for which her father and grandfather, Sir Walter and Sir Lucas, stood bound to the King by bond, in consideration chiefly of Sir Christopher's labours, and expenses incurred, when accompanying the Lord Lieutenant in various journeys. But to obtain legal possession of the seigniories accruing to him by this marriage, Sir Christopher and Lady Johanna were obliged to sue out several charters or letters patent, whereby the King forgave and remitted the penalties imposable on those who married the King's wards, or entered on their possessions, without royal licence; and accordingly Henry the Fourth, Henry the Fifth, and Henry the Sixth, granted several such pardens, now enrolled, to the said Sir Christopher and Johanna his wife, remitting all actions, penalties, and fines for this marriage, and for entering into the manors of Killeen, Kilskeer, Killallon, &c. In these records, which were tantamount to a new gift from the Crown of the seigniories, and in several others entered on the Exchequer rolls, the marriage, the estates, and the descent of Johanna from Sir Walter the grandfather, are set forth. Soon after this, Sir Christopher changed his residence to Killeen castle, where he thenceforward resided."

Geoffrey de Cusack died 1210/18
married Matilda le Petit

Adam de Cusack I died 1247/48
married Lucy de Ledwych

William died approx. 1218
married Agnes

Adam de Cusack II died 1285
married Alice

Colin

Nicholas died 1335
married Margaret

Roger

Adam de Cusack III died 1287
married Johanna de Bermingham

Margaret de Cusack
married in 1304 Sir Richard de Tuit I

Richard de Tuit II
married Blanche Butler

Joan de Tuit
married Sir Walter de Cusack died 1402

Richard de Tuit III died 1305/51

Geoffrey

John

Joan married
John Bermingham

Luke de Cusack died 1388
married Maud Flemming

Joan de Cusack

DE CUSACK

The Cusack family originated in, and took its name from Cussac, a small town (or its castle) situated in the old Duchy of Aquitane, or Guyenne, as it was called later, in south-western France. Geoffrey de Cusack appears to have come over from France to assist Hugh de Lacy in colonising Meath in about 1175.

Killeen remained in the de Cusack family until 1304 when Margaret de Cusack, heir of Adam III, married Richard de Tuit I. When Richard de Tuit III died 1350/1351 without leaving an heir, his sister Joan succeeded. Sir Walter de Cusack married Joan de Tuit in the 1340s and became lord of Killeen and Clonee, by right of his wife. Sir Walter was from Gerardstown, parish of Kilcarne, barony of Skryne. Sir Luke de Cusack inherited Killeen on his mother's death, his parents having had their marriage dissolved, and many bitter disputes ensued. He was knighted before 1382 and died shortly after September, 1388, having married Matilda, (Maud), daughter of Sir Simon Fleming, and left an only child, Joan, who married Sir Christopher Plunkett in 1402. From then on the name Plunkett became synonymous with Killeen.

The Irish Genealogist featured several articles on the Cusack Family of Counties Meath and Dublin by Hubert Gallwey and they refer to their arrival, down to the failure of the senior line of Killeen, Co. Meath, their principal fief. However, there were many "cadet" branches of the Cusacks.

Within the Killeen Manor three castles are charted, Killeen, Dunsany and Corbally (thought to be the castle of Cusack of Belpere).

BARONS OF DUNSANY

1410	1462	1st Baron of Dunsany Christopher	First married Anne, daughter of Richard Fitzgerald of Ballysonan, Co. Kildare. Second married Elizabeth, sister of 1st Viscount Gormanstown, Co. Meath.
	1482	2nd Baron of Dunsany Richard	Married Joan, daughter of Sir Rowland FitzEustace.
	1500	3rd Baron of Dunsany John	Married Catherine, daughter of Hussey, territorial Baron of Galtrim, Co. Meath.
	1520	4th Baron of Dunsany Edward	Married Anne, daughter and heir of Philip de Bermingham.
	1556	5th Baron of Dunsany Robert	First married Eleanor, daughter of Sir William Darcy, Platten, Co. Meath. Second married Genet, widow of Alderman Shillengford, daughter of William Sarsfield.
	1564	6th Caron of Dunsany Christopher	Married Elizabeth, daughter of Sir Christopher Barnewall of Crickstown, Co. Meath.
	1601	7th Baron of Dunsany Patrick	Married Mary, daughter of Sir Christopher Barnewall of Turvey, Co. Meath.
	1603	8th Baron of Dunsany Christopher	Married Maud, or Madeline, daughter of Henry Babington, Dethick, Derby.
	1668	9th Baron of Dunsany Patrick	Married Jane, daughter of Sir Thomas Heneage of Haynton, Co. Lincoln.
	1668	Edward	Married Catherine McDonnell, daughter of 1st Earl of Antrim.
	1690	10th Baron of Dunsany	Grandson of Patrick, unmarried.

	1735	11th Baron of Dunsany Randal	First married Anne, widow of 1st Earl of Carlingford, and daughter of Sir William Pershall, Suggenhill, Co. Stafford. Second married Bridget, only daughter of Richard Fleming of Stahalmock, Co. Meath.
1713	1781	12th Baron of Dunsany Edward	Married Mary, daughter of Francis Allen of St. Wolstan's, Co. Kildare.
1738	1821	13th Baron of Dunsany Randal	First married Margaret, widow of Edward Mandeville of Ballydine, Co Tipperary, and daughter of Edward Archdekin, Co. Kilkenny. Second married Emma Mary, daughter of John Smith, London.
1773	1848	14th Baron of Dunsany Edward Wadding	First married Charlotte Louisa, daughter of 1st Baron Cloncurry. Second married Eliza, daughter of the 7th Lord Kinnaird.
1804	1852	15th Baron of Dunsany Randal Edward	Married Elizabeth, daughter of Lyndon Evelyn of Keynsham Court, Co. Hereford.
1808	1889	16th Baron of Dunsany Edward	(Brother of Randal) Married Anne Constance Dutton, daughter of 2nd Baron Sherborne, Gloucestershire.
1853	1899	17th Baron of Dunsany John William	Married Ernle Elizabeth Louisa Maria Grosvenor, daughter Col. Francis Augustus Plunkett Burton.
1878	1957	18th Baron of Dunsany Edward John Moreton Drax	Married Lady Beatrice Child-Villiers, daughter of 7th Earl of Jersey.
1906	1999	19th Baron of Dunsany Randal Arthur Henry	First married Vera, daughter of Dr. Genesio de Sa Sotto Maior. Second married Sheila Victoria, daughter of Captain Sir Henry Erasmus Edward Phillips.
1939		20th Baron of Dunsany Edward John Carlos	Married Maria Alice de Villela de Carvalho

THE DUNSANY PLUNKETTS' FAMILY TREE

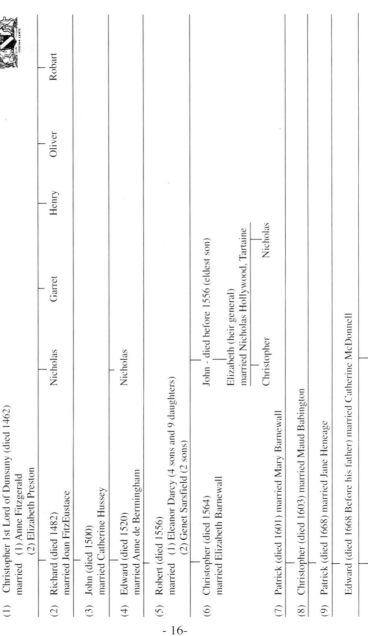

(1) Christopher 1st Lord of Dunsany (died 1462)
married (1) Anne Fitzgerald
         (2) Elizabeth Preston

Nicholas   Garret   Henry   Oliver   Robart

(2) Richard (died 1482)
married Joan FitzEustace

(3) John (died 1500)
married Catherine Hussey

(4) Edward (died 1520)
married Anne de Bermingham

Nicholas

(5) Robert (died 1556)
married (1) Eleanor Darcy (4 sons and 9 daughters)
         (2) Genet Sarsfield (2 sons)

(6) Christopher (died 1564)
married Elizabeth Barnewall

John - died before 1556 (eldest son)

Elizabeth (heir general)
married Nicholas Hollywood, Tartaine

Christopher   Nicholas

(7) Patrick (died 1601) married Mary Barnewall

(8) Christopher (died 1603) married Maud Babington

(9) Patrick (died 1668) married Jane Heneage

Edward (died 1668 Before his father) married Catherine McDonnell

(10) Christopher - (died 1690) unmarried

(11) Randal (died 1735)
married (1) Anne Pershall
(2) Bridget Fleming

(12) Edward (died 1781)
married Mary Allen

(13) Randal (died 1821)
married (1) Margaret Archdekin
(2) Emma Mary Smith

Bridget
married Hugh McGuire

Rose
married Marquess de Carondelet

(14) Edward Wadding (died 1848)
married (1) Charlotte Louisa Lawless
(2) Eliza Kinnaird

Randal
died 1835

Daughter

Daughter

Daughter

Daughter

(15) Randal Edward (died 1852)
married Elizabeth Evelyn

(16) Edward (died 1889)
married Anne Constance Dutton

Emily Valentina
married George Price

Horace
Curson

Edward
Reginald

Mary
Sophie Liza

Constance
Lavinia
Harriet

Julie
Elizabeth

(17) John William (died 1899)
married Ernle Elizabeth
Louisa Marie Grosvenor

Randal Edward Sherbourne
Eldest Son (died 1883)
unmarried

Reginal Aylmer
Ranfurly Drax
married Kathleen Quinton Chambers

(18) Edward John Moreton Drax (died 1957)
married Beatrice Child-Villers

(19) Randal Arthur Henry (died 1999)
married (1) Vera de Sá Sotto Maior
(2) Sheila Victoria Philips

Beatrice

(20) Edward John Carlos
married Maria Alice deVillela de Carvalho

Oliver

Randal

CHRISTOPHER, 1st BARON OF DUNSANY

The Dunsany estate came into being as a separate entity from Killeen when Christopher's father, Sir Christopher, and his mother, Joan, decided to divide up their property amongst their sons or marry them to heiresses! In the ensuing division, John became heir to Killeen and Dunsany fell to Christopher. According to legend the brothers agreed that the boundary between their lands should be decided by contest where two runners, wives of the brothers, would meet, one starting from Killeen and one from Dunsany. The Killeen representative had downhill momentum and was distinctly the winner.[1]

Christopher, the first Plunkett Baron of Dunsany, who was twice married, died at the comparatively early age of 52. He was styled "Dominus de Dunsany" in 1438, and created a baron by writ 17th of Henry VI in 1462 and destined to be first of twenty Barons of Dunsany to date.

[1] Mary Plunkett (sister of Horace Plunkett) writes to her nephew, Edward, recalling this event and states, "I believe it to be absolutely true, my father having received it as family history".

(It is suggested in the articles on the Cusack Family that Dunsany came into the Plunkett Family through the alliance with Anne Fitzgerald. John Cusack of Little Derricks, near Dunshaughlin, Co. Meath, and his wife Alice had a daughter Katherine, who married Sir Nicholas de Castlemartin and had a son Nicholas [living 1384], whose daughter Joan, married first Richard Fitzgerald, son of the 5th Earl of Kildare, and had a daughter, Anne, who married Sir Christopher Plunkett and brought him Dunsany).

When he carried his bride, Anne Fitzgerald, across the threshold, the stone building at Dunsany was rather primitive with four sentinel towers flanking a central courtyard. Anne apparently was a strong-minded woman, if credence can be ascribed to the story that, following a disagreement with her in-laws in Killeen, she instigated the building of her own place of worship at Dunsany: one foot longer, one foot wider and one foot higher than the "abbey" at Killeen. Whatever the motivation, Christopher and she built the Church of St. Nicholas at Dunsany and endowed it richly.

Christopher, after Anne's death, married Elizabeth Preston. His will,[2] which is preserved in the Lambeth Place Museum, London, would seem to indicate that here was a man of purpose and indeed integrity.

Christopher died in 1462 and, in accordance with his will, was buried in Killeen. It is thought that the Church in Dunsany was not completed until 1463.

[2] WILL OF SIR CHRISTOPHER PLUNKETT OF DUNSANY

"Made the day of St. Peter ad Vincula, 2 Edw. IV (1st August, 1461). His body to be buried in the chancel of Killeene before our Lady.

"Item, I will that my wife Elizabeth Prestoune have all her kine, the sheep, the stud, that I gave her, that all be clear her own. Item, I will that she have all her own plough capills and her corn of Bedlowystoune and the swine of Donsany.

"Item, I will that all mine own kine, swine, capills, and corn that is at the Clone and half my corn, capills, that bethe at Donsany, and all my rent that can be found in my tenants' hands, that all this, by the oversight of my wife and the vikery (vicar) of Killeene, bury me and inter me, and pay 19 marks and 10s to the college of Killeene, the which I oweth them; and to pay at my burying to priests at Dyvelinge and Drowdath, for masses, 20 marks.

"Item, I will, the old hanging of green and white bide in the hall at Donsany. Item, I will that the red bed, (and) a hanging of red, abide in the much chamber. Item, I will that two long costerys of red be y-given to the chancel of Donsany. Item, I will that my wife have the new bed of red and two red curtains, and the much red bed, and the little red bed, and the bed of green and red and white. Item, I will that the bed of arras and the helinge (sic) of the bed, be y-given to the Church of Donsany. Item, I will that the furnace and the lead abide to mine heir in the place of Donsany, with morell (sic) the black pot. Item, I will that all other harness of household help to bury me.

"Item, as touching my silver vessels, I will that my wife have a basin and laver of silver, a pot of silver, a standing piece of silver over-gilt. Item, the high pensill piece of silver over-gilt, with a lure, the borders gilt, with a standing foot, a harness morrane, and a plain piece of silver. Item, I leave the t'other part of my silver vessel[s], massery, mornanys to make two censers and a cross of silver over-gilt; and what cometh over that, to pay my debts and to bury me.

"Item, I will that my niece Joan have my scarlet gown and the fur. Item, I will that all mine other gowns be delivered to priests.

"Item, (of) all my silver vessels, I will that my wife make two censers, a cross, a chalice over-gilt, to the church of Donsany, and to have that for my silver vessel (sic).

"Item, I owe to the college of Killeene 19 marks and 10s. Item, I will that the Midsummer rent of Cloney, of anno Ed.2, (sic), pay Foyle of Dwilinge, merchant, 5l. 14s. Item, I owe Robert Whitt of Dwilinge, 32s. Item, I owe Browne of Drowdath, 7s. 4d. Item, I will that Awly O'Doffermoth have two marks, for hides that I had of him.

"Item, I leave to the church of Donsany the 4 antiphoners, 3 gradalys, 3 mass books, a legend, 2 sawters and hymners y-noted; with these, the sawter's epistolary, a versiculary, and a martyrology; a cope of gold, a chasuble of cloth of gold, a chausable of red satin, the cross, and the two censers and a chalice, the which yet was with the goldsmith of Trym, the day that this was writ.

"Item, I have yeve my wife, in jointure, the Lordship of Cloney. Item, I will that mine heir have my land, as the 'tail maketh mention. Item, I will that my wife [have for] term of life, in jointure, 10 marks, in the lordship of the Old-castle. Item, I will that Richard, Nicholas, Garrett, Henry and Oliver, have the lands as her (sic) 'tail maketh mention.

"Item, I will that Garrett Plunkett make an end with John Avelle, and with Betaghe's daughter, the which [is] his wife, about the two serchalls that is betwixt Luthencrue and the Old-castle, for I suppose her right is best; and I discharge me, and charge Garrett, to end with him.

"Item, I leave St. Nicholas' church of Donsany 100s. in the Miltoune, besides Prestoune; in the day of the writing it borne (sic) 4 marks; John Tanner and John Ludwiche, tenants of it. Item, I leave to the said church the mill of Alomny, bearing a year to Sir Nicholas Barnwell his wife, while she liveth; and 8 acres of land clear to the church. Item, I leave to the said church the paas (sic) in Fyngall. Item, I leave to the said church 5 marks, the which I received yearly in Thomaztoune, for the certain that I sawe (sic) to the Earl of Ormond, for the 5 marks in Thomaztoune. And I will that my wife have all the rule of the said livelihood that shall go to the church of Donsany, to find priests to pray for me, until that time that my wife and my friends mortifies by a great parlement the aforesaid livlihood to priests, to sing at Donsany for Anne Fitzgerald, that was my wife, and for Elizabeth that is my wife, and for myself. And which of my children that breaketh my will, I leave him Christ's curse, and mine; and all that helpeth to fulfil my will, I leave him my blessing.

"Item, I will that the stud that is wone (sic) of Coffy be dealt in six parts, that is to say, to my five sons, and to John mine heir. Also my son Robart Plunkett saith that

Anne Fitzgerald, that was wife, should have yew (given) him an ouch, a pot of silver, and a much cope of silver of mine; and I deny, for I grant nought thereunto, for he never pleased me. And, as I am thus advised, I will that Oliver Plunkett have Thomas -Brydistoune, besides Moylaghts, and know that is my will.   I will that Elizabeth, my wife, have - and she to do for my soul, the bawdrick of coral, the ouches, and rings that I gave her.

"Item, Anne Fitzgerald and I left to our Lady of Donsany the great red chaplet of pearls.

"Also I will Sir Robert of Prestoun and my brother Thomas Plunkett[3] help and see that my will thus y-writ may be fulfilled; and so for beds, girdles, and all other small harness, the which I gave my wife Elizabeth, I will that she have them; and to the which will I putteth to my seal of arms."

[3]Thomas Plunkett, Christopher's brother, was appointed Chief Justice of the King's Bench in 1461. Thomas resided in Rathmore, Co. Meath.

RICHARD, 2nd BARON OF DUNSANY

Richard Plunkett married Joan, daughter and co-heir of Sir Rowland FitzEustace, Baron Portlester (by Margaret, daughter of Jenico Dartois), Lord Treasurer of Ireland in 1471 and Lord High Chancellor in 1474.

Richard was living 17th June 1477, but died circa 1482.

"At the time of the Wars of the Roses in England, an Edward Plunkett, a member of a prominent Meath family, [quite possibly a member of the Dunsany family], was arrested and imprisoned in February 1468, along with the earls of Desmond and Kildare on the instructions of the chief governor, Sir John Tiptoft, 'the butcher', and charged with treason. Four days later Desmond was taken out and beheaded. Desmond's summary execution amazed and shocked almost all sections of Irish society. The official reason for Desmond's execution, given in the statute that convicted himself, Kildare and Plunkett of treason, was that he had breached the Statute of Kilkenny of 1366 by his 'alliance with the Irish enemies of the king, as in giving to them horses and harnesses and arms and supporting them against the king's faithful subjects'. Plunkett and Kildare had been convicted of the same offences but did not share Desmond's fate. A story preserved in the Desmond family, states that Desmond's death was caused by the vindictiveness of Edward IV's queen, Elizabeth Woodville, who knew he had condemned the king's marriage to a lady of so mean a house and parentage."

The Annals of the Four Masters record that in 1474 Edward Plunkett, the very best of the English of Meath, died.

JOHN, 3rd BARON OF DUNSANY

John, who in 1472 had been one of the thirteen knights of the Irish Order of St. George, succeeded to the title of Baron of Dunsany on the death of Richard, c. 1482.

On 25th May 1488, he was granted a general pardon along with six other Irish Lords, probably in connection with Lambert Simnel's conspiracy.[1]

He sat in the parliament of 1490 and 1493 and being summoned to the parliament which met at Castledermot, 26th August 1498, was fined 40s. for non-appearance.

He married Catherine, daughter of Hussey, territorial Baron of Galtrim. John and Catherine are accredited with a late medieval manuscript[2] now in the Bodleian Library, University of Oxford.

John was renowned for his scholarship in an illiterate age. He died about 1500.

[1](William Lynch in *The Ancient Baronage of Ireland*, 1829, records that King Henry VII, in the year 1489 and after the suppression of Simnel's rebellion, summoned all the Temporal Peers of Ireland, then fifteen in number, to meet him at Greenwich; there to receive at once his reprimand and his pardon for the support which they had afforded to that imposter. He then invited them to a magnificent entertainment, at which he caused Simnel to wait as a menial. Plunkett of Dunsany attended.)

[2] This medieval Meath manuscript is fragmentary, bound and now consists of 154 vellum leaves; many of the original pages are missing. It was written by Sean O'Maoilchonaire for the 3rd Baron and his wife in the house of Angus O'Dalaidh and his wife, the daughter of Pilib O'Gibne, in the closing years of the fifteenth century. (Sean O'Maoilchonaire died while on his bardic circuit in 1489.) By 1560 the manuscript was in the house of Sir Christopher Barnwell at Crickstown, Co. Meath. Most of the surviving leaves contain an Irish translation of the Quest for the Holy Grail.

EDWARD, 4th BARON OF DUNSANY

Edward married Anne, daughter and heir of Philip de Bermingham.

He fought in the famous battle of Knocktoe (about eight miles north-east of the town of Galway), in August 1504. This battle, with heavy casualties, was the scene of the Earl of Kildare's most famous triumph.

In 1521, when a much older man, he went to Killaderry in Co. Offaly and pursued the outlawed O'Carroll and O'Connor. The latter suddenly turned around and killed the knight, who was brought home and for some inexplicable reason buried in the church at Killeen.[1]

The exact date of his death was 24th January, 1521.

---

[1] The tombstone is quite plain except for an inscription around the edge in large letters in Latin. The translation is:

> *"Here lies the bodies of Sir Edward Plunkett Kt,*
> *Lord of Dunsany, who was slain at Killaderry in Offaly*
> *in the time of the Earl of Surrey, Deputy of Ireland,*
> *in AD 1521, and of Any Bermingham his wife, AD 1500"*

ROBERT, 5th BARON OF DUNSANY

Robert was one of the peers of the parliament held at Dublin in 1541, when he ranked immediately after his kinsman, Lord Killeen.

An order for his attainder was issued about November 1535. On 29th April 1537, he is reported by the Irish Council to Cromwell as "neither of wisdom nor activity" and as keeping no men to defend the marches against the Irish. He was granted pardon (together with Christopher Plunkett of Oldcastle, esquire) as Robert Plunkett Knt, Lord Dunsanye of Dunsany dated 7th April 1549, and in December of that year was a member of the Irish Council. He first married Eleanor, daughter of Sir William Darcy, of Platten, Vice-Treasurer of Ireland. She was living in 1516. They had four sons and nine daughters.

He second married Genet[1] (widow of Alderman Robert Shillengford, daughter of William Sarsfield, Alderman of Dublin), with whom he had two other sons. He died in 1556.

---

[1]His widow married James Luttrell (son and heir apparent of Sir Thomas Luttrel of Luttrellstown), who died 30th April 1557. She fourth married Sir Thomas Cusack, ·sometime Lord Chancellor. Genet married, fifth before 1579, Sir John Plunkett of Dunsoghly, Co. Dublin, Chief Justice of the Queen's Bench 1562, till his death 1st August 1582 one of the prime assistants of Elizabeth in establishing the Protestant religion in her Irish Dominion. Genet's sixth husband was Sir John Bellew of Bellewstown and this fact explains her interment at Moorchurch near Julianstown, Co. Meath. On a stone, now built into a wall of the old pre-Reformation church, the inscription reads:

An elaborately decorated stone (pictured below) from Genet's house in Jervis Street may be seen in Dunsany Castle.

(Photograph: Paul Tierney)

"Here under Lyeth
The Body of Dame Janet
Sarsfield
Lady Dowager of Dunsany
Who died XXIIII of
February,
An.Dni. 1597".

According to tradition, she was the tallest woman in Ireland. A doorway in Dardistown Castle, altered to accommodate her great height, can still be seen there.

CHRISTOPHER, 6th BARON OF DUNSANY

Second,[1] but first surviving, son and male heir. Christopher married Elizabeth, daughter of Sir Christopher Barnewall of Crickstown. He died between 29th May 1564 and 28th August 1565.

His widow married O'Reilly. "The great O'Reilly married my mother" wrote Patrick, 7th Baron of Dunsany to Robert Cecil in 1600.

[1] Elizabeth, his niece, who married Nicholas Hollywood of Tartaine, Co. Dublin, was the heir general, being daughter and heir of John Plunkett, the first son of the 5th Baron, who died before 1556. The visitation certificate of her husband has survived and reads: "Mr. Nicholas Holywood of Tartaine in the County of Dublin, Gent, being sonn and heire of Thomas aforesaid, married Elizabeth the daughter of John Plunkett, Lord of Dunsany, in the County of Meath and hath issue by her two sonnes, Christopher and Nicholas."

PATRICK, 7th BARON OF DUNSANY

Patrick was left as a minor and his wardship was granted by Privy Seal, 1565, to Sir Christopher Barnewall of Turvey, whose daughter Mary he afterwards married.[1] (She was the eleventh-youngest daughter of his guardian by Marion, daughter of Lawrence Sherle of Shallon, Co. Meath.)

Patrick was educated in the grammar school at Ratoath, under the direction of a master named Staghens. He became renowned as a person of learning, and set a standard for learned men.[2] He was one of the Masters of the Guild of the Virgin Mary of Killeen.

During the rebellion of the Earl of Desmond (1574-82) he appears to have been disaffected to the English Government. He sat in the parliament of 1585, was appointed Governor of the barony of Kells, Co. Meath, in 1599 by the Earl of Essex and took an active part against the Irish rebels in 1600.

---

[1] By indenture dated 10th February, 1572, between Patrick and his guardian, it was declared that, the said Sir Christopher Barnewall (having the wardship of his lands), "had not only bestowed the whole upon him, but also over and above had disbursed for him the sum of £430, and besides did give to him, his wife, and their issue, at the time of their entry into Dunsany, 37 Kyne and 10 calves, 15 oxen, 100 sheep, 53 swine and 3 mares; and 9 mares to be increased for the use of his son Christopher Plunkett over and above such cattle as died at Dunsany, which the said Sir Christopher Barnewall put there for their use; all of which he remitted to his Lordship by this indenture, and also the said debt; in consideration whereof and the manifold good turns done to him by the said Sir Christopher, he does covenant and agree with him fairly, for the advancement and preferment of one of the daughters of the said Sir Christopher without any further consideration, that Christopher Plunkett his son shall marry and take to wife, when he shall be required by the said Sir Christopher, or his wife Maryon Sherle, or by his heir, Patrick Barnewall."

It is recorded that "Among those employed (circa 1600) to murder O'Neill (the celebrated Earl of Tyrone) in cold blood, were Sir Geoffrey Fenton, Lord Dunsany, and Henry Oge O'Neill, but they all failed".

One of the treasures still in the possession of the Dunsany family is a mug presented by Elizabeth I, probably to Patrick, who in view of his friendship with the Queen, was dubbed by the family "a sort of small Essex". A Latin book dedicated to Patrick, dated MDLXXXIIII (1584) is still housed in the library at Dunsany Castle. (See facing page)

The 7th Baron died 1601/2.

[2] Patrick showed a marvellous command of English in his pleading letters, first to Lord Burghley and later to Sir Robert Cecil. The first letter in the Hatfield papers dates from 1575 and appeals for aid from Queen Elizabeth, "being a beggar and no chooser" but the most impressive letters date from 1596. The Queen had granted him an additional 20 horsemen and a pension to support them, but things had not gone well and he requested £400 "in consideration of the death of [his] brother, slaughter of [his] kindred and waste of [his] whole patrimony".

Just over a year later in July, 1597, he wrote again: "Having no other shield against beggary but Her Majesty's goodness, nor other passage to come thereby but through your noble favour, I beseech you to descend a little from the height of your great affairs to the due consideration of what is meet to be done for a poor gentleman in the distress I am. I have long relied upon the expectancy of her Majesty's promised goodness. Many that have been traitors, many rebels, and very many opposite to the proceedings of her Majesty, have been, and are daily, restored, relieved and employed in my country by her Majesty's pleasure.

"What a share is it, therefore, for me, having been here these four and twenty years without committing any trespass and not omitting the duty of an honest man, to be in worse case than they. Think of it, good Mr. Secretary". But the Queen did not dispense cash readily or rapidly, and later he wrote, "I am ashamed to go without some token of her Majesty's goodness, whereby I may be freed from the hateful imputation of a man either suspected and despised, being both worse than hell. Though with empty hands a man may lure no hawks, nor procure to be followed without appearance of hopes, yet I would not doubt with a little hastening to quiet all the border upon the County of the Cavan".

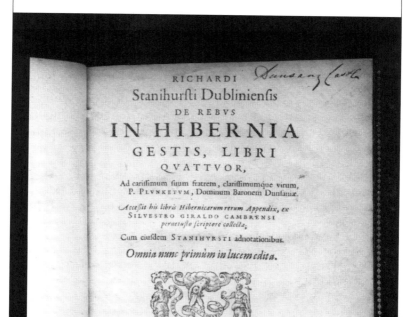

The Latin book dedicated to the 7th Baron of Dunsany

(Photograph: Paul Tierney)

- 31 -

CHRISTOPHER, 8th BARON OF DUNSANY

According to family tradition, Christopher Plunkett was involved in the Babington Plot to free Mary Queen of Scots in 1586. The group of conspirators included many young Catholic gentlemen of good standing: gallant, adventurous and daring in defence of the Catholic faith in its time of stress, ready for any arduous enterprise whatsoever that might advance the common Catholic cause. Upon discovery of the plot Christopher hastily returned to Ireland; he subsequently married (before 1595) Maud or Madeline, a daughter of Henry Babington of Dethick, Co. Derby, a kinsman of the ill-fated Anthony Babington. Christopher Plunkett[1] did not keep the condition imposed by the covenant of his father to marry and take as wife one of the daughters of Sir Christopher Barnewall.

He died shortly after his father on 15th December, 1603, and was buried at Dunsany.[2]

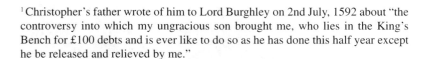

[1] Christopher's father wrote of him to Lord Burghley on 2nd July, 1592 about "the controversy into which my ungracious son brought me, who lies in the King's Bench for £100 debts and is ever like to do so as he has done this half year except he be released and relieved by me."

[2] His widow retired to Castleknock, Co. Dublin, and was murdered on the 19th March, 1609, for which crime a hired servant named Honora ny Caffry was burned at the stake. This unfortunate creature was the victim of a terrible miscarriage of justice, for not long after, a man who was to be executed for another crime confessed himself guilty of the murder of Lady Dunsany.

PATRICK, 9th BARON OF DUNSANY

Patrick was aged eight years and nine months at the time of his father's death. The 9th Baron received a patent of confirmation from James I dated 19th February, 1617, of the several castles of Dunsany, Corbally, etc. This decorative patent in Latin has survived and remains with the Dunsany family.

He married before 1634 Jane, daughter of Sir Thomas Heneage, of Haynton, Co. Lincoln.

His Lordship was subsequently summoned to the parliament of Charles I and suffered considerably in the cause of that unfortunate king. A short time before the year 1641, the Lord Justices had supplied the Lords of the Pale with arms, but suddenly recalled them, which occasioned much discontent among the Catholic Lords. Having assembled, they appointed Lord Dunsany to assure the Justices of their attachment and loyalty, and of their readiness to co-operate in every measure that would be conducive to the peace of the country. The Lord Justices, however, took no notice of this proffered service and confined Lord Dunsany in the Castle of Dublin, where he remained for several years. [1]

He was allowed (at his earnest prayer, 9th March, 1653) to plough his forefathers' fields, as tenant to the state, while waiting for transplantation; and when that day came, his wife, unable to face her bitter fate, clung with children to the castle in frenzied despair. In 1655 the Adventurers sent their agents to Ireland, and on 13th July, in that year, these agents proceeded to the Castle of Dunsany, accompanied by the High Constable and Sheriff of the county bearing the order of the Council, and demanded entrance and possession of the place for the Adventurers. "But", says Prendergast, "The Lord of Dunsany's lady denied the possession unless she was forcibly carried thence." The evictors desisted for the time being.

Next year the Adventurers came themselves. Hans Graham and others, and on 4th July, 1656, the High Constable with his force were ordered to put the Adventurers into quiet possession of the castle. Major Stanley, Justice of the Peace, was ordered to keep the peace there whilst Lady Dunsany was torn, weeping, from the scene of her former happiness and was exiled to Connaught.

On the restoration of Charles II, Dunsany regained his liberty and a portion of his property,[2] and took his seat in the House of Lords, where he continued to sit until the year 1666.

He died after May 1668 and was succeeded by his grandson.

---

[1] His apologetic letter to Ormonde, 11th March, 1642, is characteristic of the man's cringing: "Forasmuch" he writes "as by the accident of fortune, I have been involved in a business that doth trench upon my duty and credit, which is upon the general commotion of this Kingdom of Ireland. As your Lordship knows there was a great number of mistakes in the carriage of ye cause as was intimated to those who wished the same for their own particular ends, of which I was none, nor never will be.

"As for my part, I am now condemned for my slowness in following their proceedings, and am therefore at this house in dread of my life and goods. Yet I never corresponded with their councils, parleys, meetings, or camps, other than two letters, which were sent to the Lords Justices, which was for the safety of my wife and children and families, which nature leads a man unto; and the reason that made me do the same was first, I am an Englishman born, my mother an Englishwoman, and my wife an Englishwoman, the engrafting of which did alienate my heart from their cruel and base proceedings.

"And withal the ancient loyalty my house hath borne to the Crown of England being lords under the same this three hundred years, and I am the eleventh of the same family, and which times there never was any of them disloyal, and withal four of them lords of the house killed in the field in the behalf of the Crown of England and every one of the rest wounded in the same service, saving my father and myself having no occasion to be put to the same.

"And being seduced by sinister information that his Sacred Majesty did allow of this rash attempt, which was the reason of my innocent errors concerning the same; in which I did never correspond either in particular or in general, other than the present scourage did compel me to it.

"And now that I have seen his sacred Majesty's Proclamation to the contrary, I am become an humble suitor to your Lordship; that out of your accustomed favour to me, you would be pleased to accept my humble submission, to dispose of me as you will think fit; and, in the meantime, to send me your written protection and pass, being (firm) in my resolve rather to be hanged with the imagination that I died a loyal subject, and a lover of the prosperity of England, than to live in the quiet possession of all the north of Ireland".

But not all his abject protestations of loyalty, nor the reiterated assertion of his English nationality availed him, when Cromwell appeared upon the scene. He had closed the doors of Dunsany Castle as well as his ears and his heart to the call of his country, until at length he had to listen to the Usurper telling him begone.

[2] Like all Catholic landowners, he was not fairly treated, and for many years he was at law over the recovery of further property. Indeed, Sir William Petty, writing in 1686, gives a full account of the Dunsany's case as being the worst of its kind. A letter from the 9th Baron to Sir Edward Deering in January, 1667, describes his pitiable condition: "the God of heaven and earth knows my sad and deplorable condition; my weak and aged bed-ridden condition together with that unspeakable want few knows but myself, is cause enough why I am not there myself".

CHRISTOPHER, 10th BARON OF DUNSANY

Christopher was the grandson of Patrick; his father Edward Plunkett, who died in May 1688, had been referred to as "Tiarna Mor" or "the great Lord" and had the habit of never driving with less than six horses to his coach.

Christopher's mother was Catherine, fourth daughter of Randal McDonnell, 1st Earl of Antrim. (This is the first time the name Randal occurs in the family tree.) Randal's mother was a daughter of Hugh O'Neill, Earl of Tyrone.[1]

Christopher had a pension of £170.14s.4½d. a year as awarded in a letter to the Lord High Treasurer of England.[2]

From 1666 to 1692 there was no Irish Parliament but that of James II in 1689 (after his expulsion from the throne), and Christopher sat in this. After the Battle of the Boyne, James II fled to France. Christopher and the other loyalists retired to Limerick and it was here presumably that Christopher died in 1690.

He died unmarried and was succeeded by his brother Randal.

---

[1] In 1902 Mary Plunkett (Ponsonby) refers to "a very fine portrait of Hugh, Earl of Tyrone, painted in Rome by Titian, of which we have a wretched copy in the dining room!"

[2] "My Lord, pursuant to your Lordships letter of ye 24th October last which refers the petition of the Lord Dunsany to paying a grant to him and his heirs of ye quitt rent issuing out of ye lands in Ireland which belonged to his ancestors and are claimed by his Lordship, I have considered of the petition and ye references thereupon, and particularly the report made by Rd Chappel dept. audr dated the

10th August, 1684, and upon consideration of the whole matter I am of opinion that, in case his Matie shall think fitt to remitt unto ye Lord Dunsany the quitt rents issuing out of his lands, his Matie will be damaged in his yearly revenue of this kingdom the sume of one hundred and seventye pounds fourteen shillings and four pence halfepenny, according to the certificate given by the deputy auditor before mentioned; however considering ye loyalties and the many eminent services which (as is alleged) the family of the Lord Dunsany has performed to ye Crown of England, with the many hard and pressing circumstances of his present condition, I judge him an object worthy of his Maties royall bountye; but whether his Matie will be pleased to relieve him out of the fund of these quitt rents issuing out of that which was formerly his estate, or by any other wayes or means, I entirely submit unto his Maties gratious consideration. I remayne, my Lord, your Lordships most humble servant - Clarendon, Dublin Castle, Febry 3rd, 1685."

RANDAL, 11th BARON OF DUNSANY

Randal, adhering to the failing fortunes of James II, was outlawed on 16th April, 1691, but came within the terms of the Treaty of Limerick drawn up after the surrender of the city in the same year. Neglecting, however, the forms necessary to re-establish himself of the peerage neither he nor his immediate descendants had a seat in the House of Lords.

Some, like the Earl of Fingall, preferred exile, but Lord Dunsany, after a period in Holland, on recovering his lands lived on at Dunsany. There are no records of his means but it is likely that loyalty to the Stuarts had left him a poor man.

Randal first married Anne, widow of the 1st Earl of Carlingford and daughter of Sir William Pershall, but by that lady had no children. He second married, in May 1711, Bridget,[1] only daughter of Richard Fleming (of Stahalmock, Co. Meath), with whom he had a son, Edward.

The 11th Baron died on 16th March, 1735 and was buried at Dunsany, and was succeeded by his son.

---

[1] Bridget's mother, Mary, was the only child of Randal, Baron of Slane, and his first wife Elinor Barnwell. Mary re-married after her first husband was killed in Derry in 1689. Her second husband was Colonel Oliver O'Gara and it would appear that they had several children who were half-brothers and sisters of Bridget's. (See footnote 13th Baron of Dunsany)

EDWARD, 12th BARON OF DUNSANY

Edward was born in 1713, succeeded his father in 1735 and in the same year, conformed to the established Church in order, it is said, to save the Dunsany and Fingall property.

In August 1734 he married Mary, daughter and co-heir of Francis Allen, M.P., of St. Wolstan's, Co. Kildare. They had three children; Bridget, who married Hugh McGuire of Kelston, Rose,[1] who married the Marquis de Carondelet, and an only son, Randal.

Family history records that the Carondelets sent over a commission to Ireland to make sure that Rose was of sufficient high birth to enter their family. The Marquis was fifty and his bride twenty-five, and to the great amusement of the French Court of the day, he was a most devoted husband.

[1] Rose Plunkett is mentioned in the memoirs of Colonel St. Paul of Ewart. While he was in charge of the Embassy in Paris, during his chief's prolonged absence in England, he had to resolve a romantic issue. "La demoiselle Rose Plunkette, the youngest daughter of Lord Dunsany, being in Paris with her brother, was sought in marriage by one Captain McDonogh, for whom the said brother had a violent aversion. The young lady seems to have been nothing loth; so, to prevent her marriage, Plunkette had his sister shut up in the convent of Port Royal in Paris. She applied to the British Embassy for release, and although St. Paul exerted himself to obtain it, he received private instructions from the Foreign Office not to demand it Ministerially. (All persons who reside in any country are subject to the laws of that country, and you know that the head of a family by the French laws can, on assigning good reasons, shut up minors in a convent till they are of age.) It is satisfactory to learn that Miss Plunkett regained her liberty after some months and lived to marry, not McDonogh but the Marquis de Carondelet."

The 12th Baron of Dunsany[2] appears to have allowed the family fortunes to sink to their lowest ebb and it is thought that, at this time possession of land in Virginia, Co. Cavan, was lost, by neglecting to pay the interest on a mortgage. Dunsany Castle was not kept up and a village of squatters built itself in front of the hall door on what is called Black Island.

He died on 9th June, 1781.

[2] There is a complaining entry made in a Peerage referring to his "easy and unambitious disposition and, having a mind more suited to the calm duties of domestic life than to the busy scenes of political intercourse, he preferred living in a private station". His own estates must have been very limited. Pococke, in his Tour of 1752, refers to him as (despite the fact that he had conformed) "a Roman Catholic Lord of about £200 a year". This could explain why he did not establish his claim to the barony and take his seat in the House of Lords.

RANDAL, 13th BARON OF DUNSANY

Randal Plunkett was born in March, 1738/39. His early education was so neglected that at the age of sixteen, when he set out to seek his fortune, he couldn't write his name! However, he made a career for himself at the Court of Spain and succeeded in having the attainder reversed and so recovered his seat in the House of Lords.

As mentioned, the castle had fallen into dilapidation during his absence and it was only because of its sound roof that he decided to restore it, creating the beautiful stairwell and drawing room as well as putting in large windows. He removed the squatters' village from in front of the hall door,[1] created, by planting, earthworks and drainage, the organised view of the Park (still evident today).

The 13th Baron's time was one of recovery and may have been helped by (possibly) the inheritance from Count O'Gara[2] and his two marriages. His Lordship married, on 12th August, 1771, Margaret, widow of Edward Mandeville of Ballydine, Co. Tipperary, and daughter of Edward Archdekin, Co. Kilkenny, by whom he had two sons, Randal and Edward, and four daughters. Margaret died on 13th September, 1791.

Prior to the Rising in 1798 Randal issued a proclamation. (See over)

---

[1] By an act of parliament he had the road which ran under the castle wall diverted around the estate. This was resented by some who insisted on trespassing by using the old route but, as they tried to cross his bridge, the Lord threw them himself into the nearby river Skane!

Family history recalls that Randal was a man of unusual strength and stature, somewhat addicted to fine clothes as the remains of his wardrobe testified. He is even accused of having allowed his tailor to cut up the old family parchments to make patterns.

At the time of the rising, the Plunkett family held a consultation as to whether to defend Killeen or Dunsany against the rebels, as it was impossible to defend both. They decided upon Killeen, so Dunsany was abandoned and occupied by rebels. As they made to sack the cellar, a move which would have lead inevitably to the total destruction of the castle, the brewer who supplied the family said "Boys if you enter the Lord's cellar it shall be over my dead body". In return the family drank no beer other than that supplied by this brewery, though it was not good and so a relief when the firm eventually failed, as had the Rebellion.

The Baron second married, on 7th August, 1800, Emma Mary, the second daughter of John Smith of London, merchant banker, who brought the Meissen dinner service into the family as her dowry.

Lord Dunsany died 4th April, 1821 in Brussels, aged eighty-three. His ghost is said to have appeared on the night of his death in the archway outside the "Ghost room". His body was brought home and waked in the hall, the oldest men in the parish sitting up all night with lighted candles.

[2]Randal and Rose, and Randal's son, Edward, seem to have been the main beneficiaries of Count Charles O'Gara's will. Charles being a half-brother of Randal's and Rose's grandmother, Bridget Fleming.

However, Lady Mary Plunkett (Ponsonby) writes in 1902, in relation to Randal, "Count O'Gara left him £10,000 which, with the usual bad luck of our family, was lost in some way. My father used to say that my grandfather always believed that the money must have been hidden in some old book in the library and used some times to have a great hunt for it!"

TO THE PEOPLE OF IRELAND.

As it has not been the custom for Members of the Legislature to utter their opinions on public concerns, except in their respective Houses of Parliament, it may perhaps be deemed presumptuous and informal for any man individually to step forward in the manner I am about to do.—But as critical emergencies require extraordinary exertions, I feel it an indispensible duty to offer my advice to my deluded Countrymen, at such a moment as the present; and I must rest upon the purity of my motives to shield me from all reprehensions for so doing. Privileged as an hereditary Counsellor of the Nation, to offer my advice to my King upon any important point, I would certainly do so, with all duty and respect, whenever I felt it an incumbent duty: and shall I hesitate to speak also to the People, when both duty and humanity urge me to use my utmost efforts to rescue my Country from that ruin, with which an unfortunate delusion seems ready to overwhelm it?

At this awful crisis, our most gracious Sovereign has sent over the Marquis Cornwallis to govern this kingdom: a Nobleman of the most brilliant talents as a Statesman and a General. He has commenced his administration by an act, which affords you the strongest proof of the benevolence of his disposition; a benevolence so conspicuously blended with his military career as to render him revered in India; where he was some years since appointed Governor General, for the express purpose of settling the affairs of that extended country, then agitated as this kingdom is at present.

You cannot but have heard, that such an army has been landed in Ireland in the course of a few days past, as, with the troops which were here before the arrival of the Marquis Cornwallis, must enable him at any moment he pleases, to desolate your habitations and annihilate your families—yet, with this irresistable power in one hand, he offers you with the other, mercy and forgiveness. And this mercy is extended to you at a moment that your offences seemed to cut off all expectation for you, but the most rigorous severity. Hasten, then, my Countrymen, I beseech you, to avail yourselves of this lenity which is again willing to receive you into the bosom of the community, to pass an act of oblivion on all your past errors, and to restore you to that peace and tranquility which you have so rashly forsaken; for—you know not what illusive hopes.

Consider the misery and ruin you have already brought upon your country—the many thousands who have, in the space of a few weeks, fallen victims to the madness of Rebellion! For, can I suppose that any thing but madness could induce you to take up arms against the best of Kings, who has uniformly proved himself the Father of his People; and particularly so, in his gracious conduct to the Catholics of Ireland?— Let me conjure you to consider the wretched situation of your wives and children, even in this early state of your rebellion—but above all, consider the famine, which must be the inevitable consequence of your delaying to accept that pardon, which has been so unexpectedly and graciously offered to you.

During the whole course of my Parliamentary conduct, I have invariably shewn myself an advocate for conciliatory measures; and I pride myself on having acted as I did, because my conduct flowed from the conviction, that as a true friend to Ireland, I ought then to do so: But, my Countrymen, though I have been found amongst the most zealous of your friends, whilst I thought you deserving of support, you have now seen me amongst the foremost, and the most determined of your opponents, when it became necessary to meet you in the field to repress rebellion.

DUNSANY.

Dunsany Castle, July 2d. 1798.

EDWARD WADDING, 14th BARON
OF DUNSANY

Born on 7th April, 1773, Edward was educated at Westminster School and embarked on a military career during a very eventful period of history which included the French Revolution, subsequent Napoleonic wars, as well as the American wars. He saw service in Holland, America and Egypt, where he was seriously wounded in 1801.

He rose to the rank of Lieutenant Colonel in the Coldstream Guards.[1]

He first married, Charlotte Louisa Lawless on 20th June, 1803. She was the sister of the Lord Cloncurry who supported Lord Edward Fitzgerald in the 1798 rebellion. Edward and Charlotte were a very attractive couple and had three children; Randal, Edward and Emily Valentina (who married George Price, son of Sir Rose Price, 1st Baronet, on 18th October, 1839). Emily

---

[1] While on duty with them in France, Edward had the interesting experience of meeting an hitherto unknown relative, the Marquis of Carondelet, who was in fact a descendant of Rose Plunkett, Edward's grand-aunt. Lady Mary Plunkett (Ponsonby) records this chance meeting writing, "We have only one more tradition of the Carondelets. A generation later, during the Great War, your great grandfather in the Coldstream Guards was marching with a detachment through the north of France. Having bivouaced opposite a large French chateau in bitterly cold weather, he was surprised to see a young gentleman dressed in 'pink and green satin', after the fashion of the day, coming towards him across the snow from the chateau. He was still more surprised and embarrassed when the Marquis de Carondelet, as he turned out to be, embraced him affectionately in front of his soldiers and welcomed him as 'mon cousin'. He was then brought into the chateau and entertained sumptuously." Recorded by Lady Mary Ponsonby (Plunkett) c.1900.

died at Ellerslie, Jamaica, 30th October 1864. Charlotte herself did not enjoy good health and consequently the family spent much time in Italy. After fifteen years of marriage she died in Pisa in 1818.

Edward succeeded to the title in 1821 and proved his right to vote at the election of Representative Peers (Ireland) on 6th July, 1823. On 23rd March, 1823, he remarried, this time Eliza, eldest daughter of the 7th Lord Kinnaird. She was very wealthy and renovated the castle internally, built the lodges and farm offices, briefing the Irish architect James Sheil. Edward was appointed Lord Lieutenant of County Meath for the period 1835 to the time of his death in 1848 at the age of seventy-five.

Edward had literary tastes and is reputed to have spent considerable time reading the classics. Eliza was a formidable lady but, to her credit, she left a legacy of beautiful stonework in the buildings she had erected as well as in the internal reconstruction of the castle. She survived her husband and died at the ripe old age of eighty-four on 30th April, 1864, in Middlesex, England.

RANDAL EDWARD,
15th BARON OF DUNSANY

Randal Edward was born 5th September, 1804, in Rome. He was educated at Eton and at Christ's College, Oxford, achieving a B.A. in 1833. He was an M.P. (Conservative) for Drogheda 1835/37 and Representative Peer (Ireland) 1850/52.

He married Elizabeth on 29th December, 1838, at St. George's, Hanover Square, only daughter and heir of Lyndon Evelyn of Keynsham Court, Co. Hereford. Randal died without an heir on 7th April, 1852, at Dunsany Castle, and his brother Edward succeeded him as the 16th Baron.

His widow, Elizabeth, died 2nd April, 1875, at 18 Bolton Gardens, South Kensington, London.

EDWARD, 16th BARON OF DUNSANY

Edward was born on 29th November, 1808, at Ramsgate, Kent. He was married on 22nd September, 1846, to Hon. Anne Constance Dutton,[1] daughter of the 2nd Baron Sherborne of Gloucestershire.

Edward and Anne had four sons and three daughters and spent much of their time at Sherborne. There were two Dowager Lady Dunsanys at the time Edward inherited; his mother, who lived until 1864 and his sister-in-law, Elizabeth, who lived until 1875.

Edward was an Officer in the Royal Navy, serving against pirates in the Archipelago, 1826; served on the coast of Spain, 1835-40; Captain R.N. 1846; Rear Admiral (reserved list) 1864; Vice Admiral 1871; Admiral 1877. He proved his right to vote at the election of Representative Peers (Ireland) 13th June, 1856. The Minutes of Evidence were taken before The Committee for Privileges to whom the petition of the Right Honorable Edward Baron Dunsany of that part of the United Kingdom called Ireland, claiming a right to vote at the elections of Representative Peers for Ireland as heard on 9th June, 1854, before the Lord Redesdale. Edward was a Representative Peer (Ireland) Conservative 1864-89.

Edward was known as Admiral Lord Dunsany.

---

[1]Cromwell had given Loughcrew, near Oldcastle, Co. Meath, to the Naper family, who still reside there today. The Naper family was also related to the Duttons of Sherborne, so the Dunsany Family regarded the marriage of Anne and Edward as "an alliance of the plunderer and the plundered!"

Anne, Lady Dunsany, was a noted diarist[2] and corresponent. She and Florence Nightingale were friends, and the 'Lady of the Lamp' was frequently consulted regarding the health of members of Anne's family.

The 16th Baron had been a prudent young man. He invested in sheep farming in Co. Durham, then in coal mining there and subsequently set up a Merchant Shipping Company to transport the coal. These last two ventures proved to be extremely profitable.

---

[2]Below, dated 18th May, 1852, is her entry having arrived in Ireland, following the death of her brother-in-law, Randal Edward (15th Baron).

"Came to Dunsany by one o'clock. Nothing but a novel could describe our curious position in all its strange bearings - How beautiful the Park looked with its gorgeous rug of greens; its lights and shadows - its old 'Proud Church' and burial ground - its ivy and its wood! How comfortable and altogether desirable the deserted Castle! Truly I did 'covet', not my 'neighbour's house', but my own! We wandered about, hiding ourselves from the people assembled for the sale of carriages, farming stock, etc. I feel uncommonly like we are the only two who have no business here! We went to bed in the empty echoing house with locked doors and a loaded gun.

"The last three fatal years have worked a grievous change - between dilapidation suffered and devastation committed. How years of misrule tell everywhere - they tell tenfold more in Ireland than they would in England. Still, my verdict would be 'beautiful without, and unredeemable within'. Lady Dunsany will, I hope, re-establish a better state of things - and I earnestly trust that, if we are both alive, the circumstances of the cast may enable us ourselves to live, comfortably (thou' most economically) in this own real and only home. If not, ours is a dreary and desorgipeuse prospect enough!"

Edward, Lord Dunsany, was an admirer of Napoleon III. He had the upholstery for the castle library modelled on the royal apartments in the Louvre, using the same silk and braid. Admiration changed to dismay when the French were beaten in 1870 by the Prussians and, subsequently, he wrote his only book, published in 1873, called *Gaul or Teuton?* sub-titled: *Considerations as to our Allies of the Future,* a study of a suitable ally for Great Britain. The conclusion was that the Teuton was considered a better ally!

Lady Dunsany died on 27th June, 1858, aged forty-one, at Sherborne and was buried there. The 16th Baron died at Hastings on 22nd February, 1889, aged eighty.

He left everything but the castle directly to his grandson, thereby not easing the boy's relationship with his father, who naturally resented being skipped.

Florence Nightingale's signature from a letter dated 13th August 1857

JOHN WILLIAM, 17th BARON OF DUNSANY

The 17th Lord Dunsany was the second[1] son of Edward. He was born 31st August, 1853. John William received a B.A. from Trinity College (1877) and an M.A. from Cambridge (1881); he was Lieutenant R.N. Artillery Volunteers and an M.P. (Conservative) for South Gloucester 1886-92. He proved his right to vote at the elections of Representative Peers (Ireland) 1890 and Representative Peers (Ireland) 1893-99.

John William married 3rd April, 1877, at St. George's, Hanover Square, London, his cousin Ernle Elizabeth Louisa Maria Grosvenor, only daughter and heir of Colonel Francis Augustus Plunkett Burton, Coldstream Guards. She was descended from James Drax, a young Englishman who, with a few hundred pounds, had sailed from the Port of London for Barbados in the late 1620's. There he had made a fortune developing sugar and slaves into a hugely profitable business. Just before the turn of the seventeenth century, the family returned to England and bought an estate in Dorset. Lady Dunsany inherited Charborough Park, Dorset in 1905. John William and Ernle Elizabeth had two sons, Edward John Moreton Drax and Reginald Aylmer Ranfurly. (Charborough Park was left to Reginald, who changed his name to Drax.)

Lady Dunsany was a cousin of Sir Richard Burton, the great traveller, scholar, writer and translator of 'Arabian Nights'. Her son and heir, Edward, may have inherited his imaginative streak from the Burton family.

---

[1]His elder brother, Hon. Randal Edward Sherborne Plunkett, M.P., for West Gloucester 1874-80, died unmarried on 25th December, 1883, at Madeira, aged 35.

John was an exceptional sportsman and was reputed to have been the best marksman in England. He was deeply interested in mechanical things and developed his own X-ray machine, which was in operation in Dunsany Castle before his death in 1899.[2] The Dunsany version of the Röntgen ray machine was given to Sevenoaks Hospital in 1918. He had acquired the right to drive the Irish Mail Train and regularly took charge of the branch line train from Dublin to Drumree, Co. Meath. He was also responsible for having the first Irish telephone system installed in Dunsany.

The Baron died after a short illness on 16th January, 1899 at Dunsany Castle, aged forty-five years.

His widow, who by Royal Licence, 20th December, 1905, assumed the names of Plunkett-Ernle-Erle-Drax, died at her residence, Dunstall Priory, Shoreham, near Sevenoaks, Kent, on 28th February, 1916.

[2]Röntgen delivered his seminal paper on the subject in Berlin in 1895.

EDWARD, 18th BARON OF DUNSANY

Edward Plunkett, 18th Baron of Dunsany, was a soldier, sportsman, poet, playwright and generous patron of the arts. He was born in London on 24th July, 1878, educated at Cheam and Eton. On leaving Eton he went to Sandhurst in 1896. He was attached to the First Coldstream Guards. His father died in 1899 and his uncle, Horace Plunkett, took over family affairs.

At twenty-one years of age, Edward went to war in South Africa. This was to be the first of two wars he fought in with distinction; the second was the 1914-18 war.

In 1901, after the Boer War, he left the army and returned to Dunsany where he pursued his sporting hobbies, enjoying shooting and hunting. He was Master of the Tara Harriers in 1902-3. He met his future wife, Beatrice Child-Villiers, youngest daughter of the Earl of Jersey, at Ascot in June 1903, when she noted in her diary, "delightful to meet but not human enough to live with". Nevertheless, they married in 1904, and Beatrice, Lady Dunsany, took charge of Dunsany Castle and its fifteen servants and together they modernised the castle, building the new wing incorporating the billiard room. They had one child, Randal.

---

[1]His exploits as a marksman and hunter have gone into folklore! On one African Safari, for example, he bagged: "3 Jackals; 4 Congoni; 4 Waart Hog; 3 Stein Buck; 6 Zebras; 1 Waterbuck; 1 Rhinoceros; 8 Impala; 5 Thompson Gazelles; 5 Grants Gazelles; 4 Hyena; 1 Lion; 1 Dik Dik; 4 Oryx; 1 Greenock; 2 Queen Stoats; 1 Hare; 1 Snake; 2 Great Bustards; 2 Lesser Bustards; 5 Guinea Fowl; 3 Red Legged Pluvers; 1 Grey Legged Pluver and 2 various birds".

Lady Dunsany's sister Mary married Thomas, 5th Earl of Longford, whose family, the Pakenhams, are well known for their literary talents.

Edward was 6 feet 4 inches tall, a teetotaller with no interest in racing or gambling. He was an expert marksman[1]; a very keen sportsman who excelled at cricket, tennis and chess[2].

The 18th Baron was renowned as a poet, author, playwright and lecturer Many writers were regular visitors to Dunsany during this period. They included W. B. Yeats, James Stephens, Padraic Colum, Oliver St John Gogarty, Lady Gregory, George Russell, Bernard Shaw, H. G. Wells and Rudyard Kipling.

His first published work, at the age of twenty-seven, was *The Gods of Pegana* in 1905. On the insistence of W. B. Yeats he wrote *The Glittering Gate*, the first of many successful plays for the Abbey Theatre[3]. He was an enormously prolific writer and is the only playwright known to have had five plays running simultaneously on Broadway.

[2]He won the chess tournament in the Tailteann Games. He was invited to represent Ireland, which he declined, but continued to play as an amateur. He participated in exhibition games, simultaneous tournaments against the champions. He drew with the grand Chess Master, C. P. Capablanca but lost to Alekhine. Lord Dunsany wrote chess problems for the *The Times* for the rest of his life.

[3]He wrote it in a few hours and it opened in the Abbey on 3rd April, 1909. The audience and press critics were very appreciative.

He befriended the Slane poet, Francis Ledwidge, assisted him with publication and finance. Ledwidge enlisted and Lord Dunsany deeply regretted his decision to join the Army. He later wrote: "Governments should not permit poets to go to war, but they always do and they always get killed. There are lots of men but very few poets".

When his ancestral cousin, Oliver Plunkett, was beatified in 1920 Edward wrote, mischievously, that he would add a halo to his signature!

In 1940, at the age of sixty and against his doctor's advice, he enlisted as a recruit for the Home Guard. He was then asked by the British Council to take The Byron Chair of English Literature in Athens[4]. Lord Dunsany lectured to capacity audiences and was so successful that he was offered The Chair of English at the University of Istanbul. However, Germany declared war on Greece on 6th April, 1941 and on the 18th the family had to be evacuated on the *SS Warzaura*[5]. This chapter of his life is described in his long poem, *The Journey*.

In 1947 he handed over his estate to his son, Randal, and spent most of his remaining years writing at Dunstall Priory, Kent, which had been left to him on the death of his mother in 1916. During this period he made three very successful and popular lecture tours to America.

---

[4]At this time Greece was not yet at war. They set out for Athens on a journey that was to take eighty-three days. Leaving London, they travelled to Glasgow where they journeyed via Sierra Leone - Cape Town - Durban - Mombassa - Cairo - Tripoli - Budapest - Istanbul, to finally arrive in Athens on 7th January, 1941.

[5]They left in such haste that Lord Dunsany could only take two hats, one on top of the other, and a walking stick. Bombers attacked their ship daily and it was with great relief they arrived safely on 24th April, at Port Said.

During a visit to Dunsany in 1957, whilst dining with Lord and Lady Fingall, Lord Dunsany became ill and was subsequently operated on for appendicitis. He never regained consciousness and died on 25th October, 1957.

The last lines penned by the "Great Man" were as follows:

"I wish to be buried in Kent in the Churchyard of Shoreham, so as to share with every one of my neighbours whatever may be coming, when dead, as I shared it through the summer of 1940, while still alive."

He was buried in Shoreham[6].

Lady Dunsany died in May, 1970.

---

[6]Ten days later a memorial service was held at Kilmessan, Co. Meath, at which, as he wished, *Crossing the Bar* was read. As the family returned to Dunsany, four wild swans rose from the water in the park and flew in formation over the castle.

THE WORKS OF LORD DUNSANY

DATE	TITLE	PUBLISHER
1905	THE GODS OF PEGANA - Tales	Elkin Mathews
1906	TIME AND THE GODS - Tales	Heinemann
1908	THE SWORD OF WELLERAN - Tales	George Allen
1910	A DREAMER'S TALES - Tales	George Allen
1912	THE BOOK OF WONDER - Tales	Heinemann
1914	FIVE PLAYS - Plays	Grant Richards
1915	51 TALES - Tales	Elkin Mathews
1916	TALES OF WONDER - Tales	Elkin Mathews
1918	TALES OF WAR - Tales	Putnam
1919	UNHAPPY FAR-OFF THINGS - Tales	Elkin Mathews
1919	TALES OF THREE HEMISPHERES - Tales	Luce (USA)
1921	IF (reprinted with PLAYS OF NEAR AND FAR)	Putnam
1922	THE CHRONICLES OF RODRIGUES - Novel	Putnam
1924	THE KING OF ELFLAND'S DAUGHTER - Novel	Putnam
1925	ALEXANDER - Three small plays	Putnam
1926	THE CHARWOMAN'S SHADOW - Novel	Putnam
1927	THE BLESSING OF PAN - Novel	Putnam
1928	SEVEN MODERN COMEDIES - Plays	Putnam
1929	50 POEMS	Putnam
1930	THE OLD FOLK OF THE CENTURIES - A Play	Elkin Mathews
1931	THE TRAVEL TALES OF MR. JOSEPH JORKINS - Tales	Putnam
1933	LORD ADRIAN - A Play	Golden Cockeral Press
1934	IF I WERE DICTATOR (The Pronouncement of the Fraud Macaroni)	Methuen
1934	JORKENS REMEMBERS AFRICA - Tales	Heinemann
1935	MR FAITHFUL - A Play	Samuel Franck
1935	THE CURSE OF THE WISE WOMAN - Novel	Heinemann
1935	UP IN THE HILLS - Novel	Heinemann
1936	MY TALKS WITH DEAN SPANLEY - Novel	Heinemann
1936	RORY AND BRAN - Novel	Heinemann
1937	PLAYS FOR EARTH AND AIR - A Play	Heinemann

1937	MY IRELAND	Jarrolds
1938	MIRAGE WATER - Poems	Putnam
1938	PATCHES OF SUNLIGHT - Auto-biography	Heinemann
1939	THE STORY OF MONA SHEEHY - Novel	Heinemann
1940	WAR POEMS (a muddle, printed while we were abroad)	Hutchinson
1940	JORKENS HAS A LARGE WHISKEY Tales	Putnam
1943	WANDERING SONGS - Poems	Hutchinson
1944	THE JOURNEY - Poem	Macdonald
1944	WHILE THE SIRENS SLEPT - Auto-biography	Hutchinson
1944	GUERILLA - Novel	Heinemann
1945	THE SIRENS WAKE - Auto-biography	Jarrolds
1945	THE DONELLAN LECTURES 1943	Heinemann
1946	THE YEAR - Poem	Jarrolds
1946	A GLIMPSE FROM A WATCHTOWER - Pamphlet	Jarrolds
1947	THE ODES OF HORACE, Translated into English Verse	Heinemann
1947	THE MAN WHO ATE THE PHEONIX - Tales	Jarrolds
1948	THE FOURTH BOOK OF JORKENS - Tales	Jarrolds
1949	TO AWAKEN PEGASUS - Poems	G Ronald (Oxford)
1950	THE STRANGE JOURNEYS OF COLONEL POLDERS - Novel	Jarrolds
1951	THE LAST REVOLUTION - Novel	Jarrolds
1952	HIS FELLOW MEN - Novel	Jarrolds
1952	THE LITTLE TALES OF SMETHERS - Tales	Jarrolds
1954	JORKENS BORROWS ANOTHER WHISKEY - Tales	Michael Joseph

Accounts of the wedding and homecoming of Lord Dunsany and Beatrice Child-Villiers. Truly Edwardian occasions, every details being recorded by medium of the written word.

BICESTER ADVERTISER
MARRIAGE OF LADY BEATRICE VILLIERS AND LORD DUNSANY (15th September, 1904, at All Saints' Church, Middleton Stoney, Oxfordshire)

The delightful weather of yesterday (Thursday) following upon the deluge of the previous day, lent a tone of gladness and happiness to one of the prettiest events that has occurred in this neighbourhood for many years - the marriage of Lady Beatrice Child Villiers, youngest daughter of the Earl and Countess of Jersey, of Middleton Park, and Lord Dunsany, of Dunsany Castle, Co. Meath. The event has been looked forward to for a considerable time with the deepest interest by all classes of the community, for the noble Earl and Countess are so well known that to eulogise their popularity would be a waste of time and space, and it was appropriate and highly appreciated that their youngest daughter should be led to the altar in the parish in which she has spent her young days, and amongst those by whom she is so greatly beloved. On entering the village one was struck by its gay and jubilant appearance, the scene being one of general rejoicing. A committee of parishioners, chief of whom were Mr. Perry, Mr. Elliott, Mr. Bliss, and Mrs. and Miss Todd, had carried out a scheme of decorations, which, added to the display of flags, etc., from individual houses, looked very pretty. The wall of the main entrance had been festooned with evergreens, whilst over the gates was erected a triumphal arch bearing the words "Happiness and long life". Among the other decorations in the village of a conspicuous character were those at the houses of Mrs. Freeman and the Misses Webster, whilst strings of flags were stretched at intervals across the roads. Coming to the church, which stands prettily secluded among the trees in the park, a number of flags hung across the drive, upon which were designs of bells bearing the words "We all with one voice wish you health and happiness". From the entrance to the churchyard to the door of the building was erected an awning, each of the supports being entwined with evergreens, whilst the path was covered with a crimson carpet. It was here where the thoughtfulness of the Earl and Countess of Jersey for the parishioners first became apparent. It was much desired that men, women and children should be permitted to view the bridal party, and for those unable to obtain an entrance to the church accommodation was provided in the churchyard. Perfect order was maintained and as admission was gained by tickets only, there was no hitch whatever in the arrangements. The church was nicely decorated, the adornment for the harvest festival being considerably augmented by Mr. Perry, the head gardener. The ceremony was fixed for 2.30, and for some time prior to this hour the carriages rolled up in numbers, bringing guests from every direction. During the assembling of these Mr. A.M. Johnson played upon the organ selections of Mendelsohn's "Songs without word." The bridal party arrived punctually to time and was met at the entrance to the church by the surpliced choir and clergy, singing the hymn "O Father all creating," the bride being led to the chancel steps by her father.

The officiating clergy were the Hon. and Very Rev. S.W. Leigh, Dean of Hereford (uncle of the bride) and the Rev. W. H. Draper (rector of Middleton Stoney). The bride, who was given away by her father, wore a dress of white satin, skirt trimmed with deep Brussels lace, flounce caught up at intervals with white chiffon roses, bodice trimmed with Brussels lace (the gift of the bride's mother), tucked chiffon yoke and court train of tucked chiffon, lined satin. Her lace veil was that worn by her great-grandmother in the year 1804 and sister. The bridesmaids were the Hon. Kathleen Annesley, Miss Buller (daughter of Sir Redvers Buller), Miss Violet Hoare, Miss Marjorie Tubb and Miss Margaret Leigh (cousin of the bride). These dresses were of white silk over pink, straw hats trimmed with roses and pink strings. There were three pages, Masters Charles and Elwyn Rice (nephews of the bride) and Master Claude Woodhouse, and they wore white satin, with Irish Lace collars and cuffs and pink sashes. "The bridegroom's presents to the bridesmaids were diamond and peridot pendants and platinum chains, and the

bride's presents to the pages, diamond and emerald shamrock pins.

The bride carried a shower bouquet of lilies of the valley, stephanotis, myrtle and smilax, the gift of the bridegroom, whilst the bridesmaids bouquets consisted of pink carnations and tuber roses, with asparagus fronds and smilax. The service was fully choral, the Psalm "God be merciful unto us" being sung as the bride proceeded to the altar rails. Here the service was concluded and after the singing of the Hymn "O perfect love", the Dean of Hereford gave an appropriate and encouraging address to the newly married pair. During the signing of the register Mr. Johnson played the "Marche Romaine", whilst the bells struck up a merry peal, and as the party left the church the "Wedding March" was played upon the organ.

The Countess of Jersey was present in the church wearing a dress of heliotrope cloth trimmed with embroidery, whilst the Dowager Lady Dunsany wore a dress of light blue silk, with lace trimmings.

A reception was held after the ceremony in the drawing room at the house, whilst a large number of tenants, tradespeople and other guests were entertained in the dining room.

Later in the day Lord and Lady Dunsany left by special train from Somerton Station for Leek Wootton House (kindly lent by the Hon. Dudley Leigh), where the honeymoon will be spent. The bride's travelling dress was of pale green cloth, green felt picture hat trimmed with dark green velvet and shaded feathers.

The house party included the Hon. Walter and Lady Margaret Rice, Earl and Countess of Longford, Viscount Villiers, Hon. Arthur Villiers, Lady Dunsany, Lieut. the Hon. Reginald Plunkett, R.N., Sir Horace Plunkett, Hon. Reginald Villiers, Mr. and Lady Caroline Jenkins, Hon. Mrs. Ponsonby, Mr. H.C. Ponsonby, Viscount Northland, Hon. George Peel, Hon. Mrs. Rowland Leigh, the Dean of Hereford and Hon. Mrs. Leigh, etc.

Among the guests were the Hon. Agnes and Hon. Cordelia Leigh, Hon. Rowland Leigh, Col. and Mrs. England, Mrs. Withington, Mrs. Slater-Harrison, Hon. Mrs. Molyneaux, Hon. Mrs. T. Parker and Miss Parker, Miss Alice Leigh, Mr. & Mrs. and the Misses Tubb, Mr. and Mrs. Fane, Mrs. Bowlby and Miss Bowlby, Mr. and Mrs. R.D. Thomas, Rev. W.H. and Mrs. Draper, Misses Draper, Mr. and Mrs. Perceval, Mr. and Mrs. Cottrell Dormer, Rev. G.E. Barnes, Col. and Mrs. Gosling, Mr. and Mrs. Keith Falconer, Rev. G.P. and Hon. Mrs. Crawfurd, Mr. and Mrs. Woodhouse, Mrs. and Mis Chinnery, Mr. and Mrs. Little, Miss Little, Rev. A. and Mrs. Welsh, Dr. and Mrs. Symes-Thompson, Mr. and Mrs. Page, Miss Page, Mr. and Hon. Mrs. George Campbell, Mr. and Miss Burchardt, Rev. A.R. Price, Mrs. Drinkwater, etc.

The massive bridal cake was made by Mrs. Goodall, the housekeeper, and was exquisite in design.

Each of the guests and ticket holders received a wedding favour in the shape of a gilt brooch representing four-leaf shamrock, with a knot of white silk.

The numerous and exceedingly valuable wedding presents were on view in the picture gallery, the following being a list:-

BRIDE'S PRESENTS
Bridegroom- Sapphire and diamond necklace, opal and diamond pendant, emerald and diamond pendant and ring, opal and silver casket, Japanese enamelled mirror and enamel boxes.
Earl of Jersey - Diamond tiara.
Countess of Jersey - Pearl necklace, Brussels lace flounce and dressing bag.
Hon. Walter and Lady Margaret Rice - Pearl and diamond brooch.
Earl and Countess of Longford - Diamond necklace
(There follows a list of a further 258 presents to the bride.)

BRIDEGROOM'S PRESENTS
Bride - Diamond Links.
Lady Dunsany - Japanese cabinet.
Sir Horace Plunkett - Japanese screen and frames.
Lieut. Hon. Reginal Plunkett, R.N. - Silver cigar and cigarette box.
Lord Sherborne - Box of card games.
Hon. Mrs. Ponsonby - Writing table.
Miss Ponsonby - Tea basket.
Capt. and Hon. Mrs. Parr and Miss Parr - Silver inkstand.
Susan, Lady Sherbourne - Clock.
Employees on Dunsany Estate - Silver.
Countess of Jersey - Lecky's Works.
Mr. T. Ponsonby - Silver bridge box.
Mr. H.C. Ponsonby - Silver cigarette box.
Mrs. Holroyd Smith - Silver fish.

Lord and Lady Dunboyne - Silver Mounted Blotter.

Duchess of Somerset - Silver paper cutter.

Lady Victoria and Hon. A. Herbert - Blotter & paper case.

Lord and Lady Bellew - Satsuma China Bowl.

Colonel and Mrs. Dutton - Connemara marble pen wiper.

Mr. Lesley Butler - Inkstand.

Mr. and Mrs. Congreve - Silver cigarette box.

Lord and Lady Borthwick - Silver Trays.

Earl and Countess of Cassilis - Silver Trays.

Col. and Mrs. Dayrell Hammond - Silver cigarette box.

Mr. T.E. Gunning - Mother of pearl and ruby links.

Mr. Bury - Barometer.

Marquis and Marchioness of Bath - Silver candlesticks.

Lady Eleanor and Miss Brodie - Silver gilt teaspoons.

Sir John and Lady Dillon - Cigar Lighter.

Hon. Mrs. Yorke Bevan - Brass box.

Mr. and Mrs. Dunbar Buller - Old Irish silver sauce bowl.

Mr. Robert S. Gardiner - Silver mounted decanter.

Mr. and Mrs. F. Verney - China Plate.

Hon. Julia Dutton - China Box.

Earl and Countess of Ranfurly - Cut glass jug and basin.

Mrs. Cleek - Bridge and piquet box.

Countess of Limerick - Shelley.

Lady May Murphy - Silver gilt spoon.

Mrs. Herbert Smith - Silver card case.

Mrs. Cordy - Ivory Brushes.

Mr. F.B. Nixon - Gold cigarette case.

Col. and Mrs. G. Napier - Leather case.

Capt. and Mrs. George E. Price - Visiting Book.

Lady Mowbray and Stourton - Tortoiseshell and silver paper knife.

Miss Barker - Ivory and silver paper knife.

Lady Hall - Bridge book.

Hon. Claud Brabazon - Silver coffee pot.

Earl of Malmesbury - Tortoiseshell and silver letter clip.

Mr. and Mrs. Poyndon Haden - Silver inkstand.

Misses Cameron - Mother of pearl handled magnifying glass.

Lord Cloncurry - Pair of silver candlesticks.

Unionists of West Wilts - Large silver bowl.

Viscount and Viscountess Powerscourt - Two silver bedroom candlesticks.

Viscount Northland (bestman) - Despatch box.

Capt. Bigham, C.M.G. - Silver mounted decanter.

Lady Beatrice Child-Villiers

Edward, Lord Dunsany

SEVENOAKS CHRONICLE - 7th November, 1904
LORD AND LADY'S DUNSANY'S HOMECOMING
ENTHUSIASTIC RECEPTION -
PRESENTATION OF ILLUMINATED ADDRESS

Lord and Lady Dunsany had a most enthusiastic reception when they returned to Dunstall Priory, Shoreham, Kent, on Monday evening, after their honeymoon trip. The villagers had decided to pay due honour to the occasion, and consequently a "Reception Committee" was entrusted with the success of the undertaking. This included the Rev. T. K. Sopwith (chairman), Mr. Isaac Loveland (treasurer), Mr. W.Tappin, Mr. G. Pocock, Mr. J. Bowers, Mr. B. Lightfoot, Mr. A. G. Bartlett, Mr. F. Cox, Mr. W. Wilson, Mr. G. Wood, Mr. S. Yates, and Mr. F. R. Robertson (secretary). Having arranged for the presentation of an illuminated address of welcome, the attendance of the Brass Band, and a torch-light procession from the railway station to the Priory, other matters were left until the day of arrival. Unfortunately the weather interfered considerably with the decorative scheme. Monday was a consistent "soaker", but the adverse elements in no way damped the ardour of the promoters. They had decided to give his lordship and his bride a fit and proper welcome to Shoreham, and that they would do in spite of the unpropitious weather. The booking-hall at the station was the centre of attraction, for it was here Lord Dunsany was to introduce her ladyship to the leading lights of the village. The place was accordingly profusely decorated. Flags, relieved with foliage, covered the bare walls, while strings of paper chains crossed and re-crossed the ceiling. Over the booking office were the crests of the two families now linked in the holy bonds of matrimony, whilst over the exit, on a ground of crimson, was the word "Welcome", in bold gold letters. These decorations were the work of Miss and Mr. Lightfoot, the daughter and son of the stationmaster. From the doorway to the end of the station approach, flags and bunting fluttered in the high wind. The station-master's house had been gaily decorated with flags and illuminated with fairy lights and Chinese lanterns, and near by was a triumphal arch, also illuminated with fantastic lights, one large lantern bearing the words "Long life and Happiness". The house opposite the approach - we understand the residence of Mr. Mildmay's steward - was also prettily bedecked and stood out prominently in the blackness of the night.

Long before the train arrived the Shoreham Brass Band was ready on the platform, - under the direction of bandmaster Booker, - the horses had been taken out of the shafts, and ropes attached, and the torch bearers had formed a procession. A peculiar feature of the affair, were the improvised drums. Mr. Samuel Cheeseman had been requested to make torches, but he went further, and getting a number of old American cheese boxes, covered them over with parchment-like papers, painted on suitable mottoes, such as

"Welcome Home", "Hearty Greetings", "He's a jolly good fellow", etc., and stuck a candle inside. They had a weird look on poles but were most effective.

As the engine steamed into the station the band struck up "Home, sweet Home", and in the distance could be heard the peal of bells from the Shoreham Parish Church. As Lord and Lady Dunsany came along the platform, accompanied by the stationmaster, the band played an Irish jig. His lordship was received in the waiting room by the Committee and then Miss Flossie Lightfoot presented Lady Dunsany with a beautiful shower bouquet from Seale's Nursery, Sevenoaks. Her ladyship, having been introduced to the members of the committee, Sergt. Humphrey made a passage through the crowd and the couple quickly took their seat in the carriage. Headed by the torch bearers and the band, the procession started for Dunstall Priory, about 20 men being at the ropes attached to the vehicle. At the entrance to the drive was another triumphal arch, and lanterns and torches were fixed at various places right up to the house, Mr. Wilson, the steward, having made every preparation at this part. Yet another arch was near the house, and over the porch was the word "Welcome", other appropriate mottoes being fixed in conspicuous places.

When the procession arrived at The Priory, the happy couple were welcomed by the Lady Dunsany and other friends. Amongst those near the porch were the Rev. and Mrs. T. K. Sopwith, Mr. I. Loveland, Mr. Lightfoot, and others.

Approaching his Lordship, the Vicar of Shoreham read the following address, -

a beautiful illuminated affair, bound with vellum:-
To the Right Honourable Lord Dunsany.

"We the undersigned, on behalf of many inhabitants of the parish of Shoreham, beg to tender to you and Lady Dunsany our hearty congratulations on the occasion of your marriage.

"We take this opportunity of expressing our sincere appreciation of the generous support which you have given to the Institution which exists in our village for the developments of the welfare, physical, mental and moral, of its inhabitants, and we venture to express the hope that you will continue to show in the future the same kindly interest in the well-being of Shoreham that you have evinced in the past.

"We trust that, under the blessing of Almightly God, you may enjoy many years of domestic happiness, and that there lies before you a long and honourable career of usefulness in the service of the State."

T. K. SOPWITH, Vicar of Shoreham.
(Chairman of Committee)

ISAAC LOVELAND, Treasurer

R. F. ROBERTSON, SECRETARY

Lord Dunsany, who was cordially received, thanked the people of Shoreham for the beautiful address, and for the hearty welcome they had accorded Lady Dunsany and himself. It was most kind of them to come out in such a wet night, as that unfortunately proved to be, and he greatly appreciated the honour himself, and he felt sure Lady Dunsany also appreciated the cordial reception and the address they had been so good to give them. He did not think there was any part of the world for which he had more affection than the village and valley of Shoreham- with its old associations and pleasant memories. It was in that valley, between those hills, that he first saw any part of England, and consequently Shoreham was amongst the first and most early recollections. He had always liked the place as his home. (Applause.) It was there he was brought up, and there that he was first taught that the world was round, and which he strongly disbelieved when he looked at the other side of the valley and saw it was not. (Laughter.) He remembered many of those present as long as he could remember anybody, and therefore it was a great pleasure to receive such a hearty welcome from them that evening. (Applause) He had not moved so much amongst them of late, yet he got to know many of them in the football ands cricket field. He had ample opportunity of getting to know them when playing at cricket, for if his side was in he spent more time in the pavilion than at the wicket. (Laughter and applause.) He hoped, however, to know them better in the future. Adverting to what they said about the prospects of his political career, he said he had only once before seen such a welcome, and that was when the people of Shoreham turned out to welcome his father back after his return to the House of Commons. It was not until then that he had some kind of aspiration to get into Parliament. He did not think there was any certainty, or much possibility of his getting returned for Parliament this time, but his intention was to try until he did get in. (Loud applause.) It had been said that the side he belonged to had not been very prosperous since Mr. Chamberlain brought forward the Fiscal question. That was no reason why he should desert his party, nor a reason why he should not persevere in his candidature. It was the duty of every man to carefully consider what was the best for their country, and whether he be Conservative or Radical, free or fair trader, or whatever he liked, he should do his best according to his lights (applause). Once more he thanked them for the hearty reception given to Lady Dunsany and himself-a reception she would always remember (applause).

His lordship then invited the large concourse of spectators to partake of refreshments, which they did, the band playing selections in the courtyard despite the downpour. There were two large marquees erected close to the house, one for the tenants and the other for the general inhabitants of Shoreham, and here "the health of Lord and Lady Dunsany" was toasted over and over again.

RANDAL ARTHUR HENRY, 19th BARON OF DUNSANY

Randal Arthur Henry was born on 25th August, 1906 at Portobello House, Dublin. Much of his childhood was spent in Dunsany. He started school at Forzie Place in England and completed his studies at Eton, then joined the Army and spent nineteen years with the Guides Cavalry in India. He also served in the Middle East.

In 1938 he married Vera, daughter of Dr Genesio de Sá Sotto Maior of San Paulo. She was reputed to be a lady of outstanding beauty. They had one son, Edward, who was born in Dublin in September 1939.

Randal had gone to war shortly before the birth of his son. Vera, with Edward, went to the U.S.A. and then Brazil. Their marriage was not to last. After the war they divorced and Randal brought back his son, leaving him in the care of his own parents.

In 1947 Randal married Sheila, daughter of Captain Sir Henry Philips. They had one daughter, Beatrice, who was born in Dublin on 15th July, 1948. Sheila, already had one daughter by her first husband, Baron de Rutzen.[1] Randal retired from the army with the rank of Lieutenant Colonel in 1947 and returned with his wife to live in Ireland, taking over the estate.

---

[1] He was killed in Italy in 1944.

Randal and Sheila took a keen interest in the Dunsany Castle Estate, investing in new machinery, new herds, land development and continuing production of their saw mill. Lady Dunsany hosted the first fashion show of the late Sybil Connolly in the billiard room in 1953.[2]

Randal was a polo player of world class. In his youth he was an accomplished horseman and master of The Tara Harriers. Later he gave up riding, took to reading history and became Grand Bailiff of the Military and Hospitilier Order of St. Lazarus of Jerusalem in Ireland.

He wished to be remembered as a professional soldier, an expert on the Middle East, and strongly believed he was descended from the Vikings. He was a homeopathist to which he attributed his longevity.

The 19th Baron of Dunsany died on 6th February, 1999, and his death was followed by his wife's on 24th July in the same year. He was buried, as he had always wished, at the top of the motte in front of Dunsany Castle.

[2]This was to launch the designer to world fame.

EDWARD, 20th BARON OF DUNSANY

Edward Plunkett, 20th Baron, artist and designer, is now in residence with his wife, the Brazilian architect Maria Alice de Marsillac Plunkett, AIA, RIBA, RIAI. They have two sons, Randal and Oliver.[1] Completing the immediate new generation are Daniel and Joana, the children of Lady Dunsany's first marriage. Daniel and Joana de Marsillac, both working in Europe at present, although they are UCD graduates.

Once again the old house echoes with youthful laughter!

[1]Maria Alice comes from an old Catholic family and has brought up her sons as such. The Plunketts, who conformed to the Church of Ireland in the early eighteenth century, now in the New Millennium, return to the faith of their ancestors.

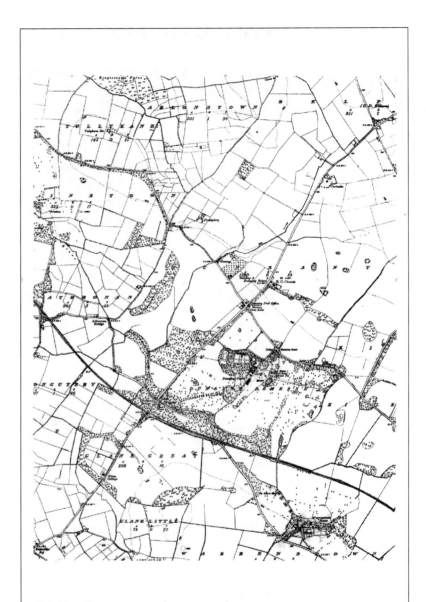

Based on Ordnance Survey Map 37, Co. Meath. Revision of 1909

DUNSANY CASTLE

Hugh de Lacy, who had been granted the land of Meath by Henry II shortly after the Norman Invasion, instigated the initial structure of the castle. Hugh de Lacy was considered a great military architect and, presumably, Dunsany Castle was built in or around 1181, at the same time as Killeen Castle.

The original castle may have consisted of a series of strong towers, with a walled enclosure (bailey), where the great hall and kitchens were situated. At one time the kitchen floor in Dunsany was taken up and the under floor was seen below, still strewn with rushes. From the initial structure a fine medieval tower-house developed. The primary purpose of the two Pale castles,[1] Killeen Castle and Dunsany Castle, was to guard the two adjacent roads. The road from Dunshaughlin ran through Killeen, crossing Tara, and heading north, and another road went to Trim, then the capital of Meath, and running close to Dunsany Castle. It took an act of parliament some centuries later to move the road and the village that had grown up beside the castle walls.

The castle has been described as "a long straggling castle with, to judge from the thickness of its walls, (for all medieval details have long disappeared in the 18th century and 19th century refacings), two fortified towers set parallel to each other, at east and west ends, and joined by a long straight range. The larger of these 'castle' blocks extends from the present front

---

[1] Most of North Leinster was known as "Plunkett Country" and there was a saying: "Travellers in Meath should beware for if they are not robbed by the Lord of Killeen, they are sure to be robbed by the Lord of Dunsany".

door of the house to its extreme west end, which is fortified by two substantial square towers, projecting from southwest and northwest corners. The second 'castle' is marked on the exterior of the present house by a large early nineteenth century mullioned window, which projects at first floor level. At the main-floor level the castle contains the library. A three-story, three-bay range links the two blocks".

Of the castle's architectural history before 1750 nothing is definite, but differences in detail on the west and east sides suggest two principal periods of alteration after that. In 1781, the 13th Baron of Dunsany inherited a rather dilapidated castle but, as the roof was sound, he set about restoring it. According to tradition he employed James Wyatt as architect, but there is no documentary proof of this assumption. The decoration of the hall and drawing room ceilings is accredited to the Dublin stuccoist, Michael Stapleton. The main staircase, rising in parallel cantilevered flights, is associated with this period too.

Further restoration took place in 1825/35. James Sheil is credited with the work carried out at this time, possibly under the direction of Eliza Kinnaird, the second wife of the 14th Baron. The existing decoration of the entrance hall, dining room and library are associated with this period.

The single-storey additions at the back of the house, which include an Edwardian billiard room, was started in 1910. Designed by George Jack, who was working in William Morris's office, the agent of change this time was the 18th Baron. The billiard room is believed to occupy the site where once stood a private oratory.

Now in the new millennium, with the 20th Baron of Dunsany at the helm, restoration work is again underway.

As soon as you enter the castle you are embraced by the feeling of a home that has been occupied and loved by generations of Plunketts.

(The 18th Lord Dunsany in a novel, *The Curse of the Wise Woman,* says of an Irish House:

"It was built by a forebear of ours who was a historical character, but it just about that time that the history of Ireland begins to be fabulous, so that it is truer to tell you merely that the house was very old. Of the period of its furniture and its fixtures I can tell you at once: it was no period at all. As chairs and such things wore out they were replaced in different generations, and the only thing that they all had in common was that they were all bought by the same family. There is a right and a wrong place for antiquity; it is right in walls, wrong in carpets, wrong too in curtains and wallpaper and hearthrugs. We had antiquity everywhere.")

The Tower Lodge

(Photograph: Paul Tierney)

The neo-Gothic arched entrance

(*Photograph: Paul Tierney*)

GATEWAYS TO DUNSANY CASTLE

The Dublin Road entrance, known as the Tower Lodge, is a handsome neo-Gothic gateway, with mock portcullis, commissioned by the 14th Baron, about 1830, incorporating the Plunkett coat-of-arms quartered with his first and second wives' coats-of-arms. From here carriages travelled up the long avenue with the castle totally obscured, until it appeared magically as the driveway ran between the old church and the motte. This entrance is no longer used, and the grass has long since grown over what was once a well-maintained driveway.

The neo-Gothic arched entrance, used for runs going via Dunsany Crossroads, was built as a folly around 1760 and gives the appearance of a ruined tower castle with adjoining archway. It was intended for use by horses, pony and traps, etc., but around 1960, was slightly widened and is now the main entrance to the castle. This is a picturesque route passing down an avenue of mature tree with the church outlined against the sky to the east. Running parallel to it is the farm entrance. This driveway is flanked by beautiful old stone walls, with an arched underpass to complete the 'walk' around the pleasure grounds without encountering the working world. There are extensive eighteenth century stone farm buildings. Sir Gilbert Scott, briefed by the 14th Baron, refaced the stables, the nearest buildings to the castle. This was done in conjunction with the nineteenth century extension to the north end of the castle.

On the Glane Road, close to the old railway bridge, is the Black Lodge used for journeys to Trim. It has a neo-Norman archway incorporating a lodge built of dark limestone. This archway also displays the Plunkett coat of arms (14th Baron) and is situated alongside the river Skane. Both this and the Tower Lodge are almost certainly the work of James Sheil, who was very active at Dunsany from between 1825-35.

The Black Lodge

(*Photograph: Paul Tierney*)

DUNSANY DEMESNE

Dunsany has three mottes; the one to the east of the castle is most likely to have been the site of the original Norman stronghold. The one immediately west of the castle creates the impression of twin dunes, and yet another motte sits further west. These last two were possibly built as ornamental features.

The open view from the front of the castle was extensively worked on at the end of the eighteenth century and it was then the ha-ha, protecting the front lawn from the intrusion of cattle, was built.

The castle has a walled garden, covering of 3.4 acres, which is entered through a beautiful wrought iron gate, circa 1906. Although it no longer provides the exotic range of fruit and hot-house produce that it did fifty years ago, it is still very much a working garden and the castle has an all-year-round supply of vegetables.

Within the grounds, on the west side of the castle, is an icehouse which acted as a refrigerator and store for the house.

The river Skane flows through the Railway Wood where the Dublin-Navan line was active for over one hundred years.

There are a large variety of trees and shrubs in the surrounding parkland, woods and an old flower garden that was maintained up till 1950. Forestry is an activity that is ongoing with planking of mature trees for construction and repair.

With fields bounded by woods, this is a wonderful wildlife habitat. Herons, moorhens, pheasants, sparrow hawks, kestrels, owls and jays, along with many other species of birds are apparent, not to forget the foxes, hares, rabbits, squirrels, badgers, otters and deer.

Entrance to the walled garden
(Photograph: Joan Flynn)

Old Flower Garden, Dunsany Castle

© Lord Dunsany

FIELD NAMES, WOODS & RIVERS RELATING TO DUNSANY CASTLE DEMESNE

FIELD NAMES:

11 Acres
Ash Field
Back Lawn
Barrack Field
Big Glane
Big Mullagh
Brabazon's Field
Bull Field
Chapel Field
Church Field
Cow Field
Cricket Field
Dairy Field
Derman's Field
Dispensary Field
Front Lawn
High Field

Little Glane
Low Field
Maguire's Field
Mill Field
Moore's Field
Narrow Corner
Night Field
Ox Park
Peter's Field
Pigeon Field
Pump Field
Quarry Field
Quinn's Field
Rankin's Field
Small Mullagh
The Orchard
Toomey's Field

Watch Field
Well Field
White Field

WOODS:

Athronan Woods
Clusker Woods
Duck Pond Woods

Horseshoe Woods
Laurel Woods
Railway Woods

RIVERS:

River Gansey

River Skane

The Church of St. Nicholas

(Photograph: Paul Tierney)

DUNSANY MANORIAL CHURCH

The ruined church within the demesne of Dunsany Castle was named after St Nicholas of Myra, and intended as a place of worship for the Baron of Dunsany and his family, his relations, retainers and tenants. St Nicholas is Patron of Lepers and it is possible that this dedication indicates a leper hospital in the parish, as Knights of St John of Jerusalem very often ran these Leprosaria. St Nicholas's commonest Feast Day is the 17th August; this is the Patron Day of Dunsany and, of course, he is the forerunner of Santa Claus.

The church was situated by the motte (this was a traditional location) north-east of the castle, probably on the site of the Church that was here as early as 1302-6 built by Nicholas Cusack, and was rebuilt in the middle of the fifteenth century by Christopher, the first Plunkett Lord of Dunsany, and his wife.

Measurements of church:
129 feet long
Chancel 21 feet 3 inches wide by 51 feet long
Nave 21 feet 5 inches wide and 55 feet 6 inches long
Arch is 10 feet wide. Gable is 5 feet 7 inches thick

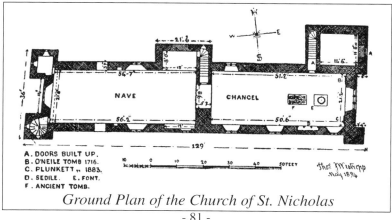

Ground Plan of the Church of St. Nicholas

The three Plunkett churches at Killeen, Dunsany and Rathmore have been well documented as they are fine examples of the late-middle ages design and ancestry and almost certainly the work of Anglo-Irish masons.

The building of the church at Dunsany seems to have been hastened due to a quarrel between the sisters-in-law in Killeen and Dunsany. Lady Dunsany is said to have declared that she would never set foot in Killeen Church again, but would build herself another church at Dunsany, similar in every respect except that it was to be a foot larger in height, length and breadth. The story has long been believed though the family thought it wiser to leave the measurements unchecked!

Christopher Plunkett, who together with his first wife, Anne Fitzgerald, built this church, donated many valuables to it as detailed in his will dated 1461.

The interior is a long rectangular space divided by one heavy circular chancel arch. Immediately west of this arch the side-walls are designed to accommodate lateral chapels; the one on the south is very shallow, but on the north side quite deep where the nave wall is projected on the exterior to provide space. A muralled staircase is located within the masonry on the north jamb of the chancel arch and rises to what was a broad gallery above the north side chapel. It is entered by pointed doorways in the north and south walls. There are two ambries (niches) just in front of these entrances for storing sacred utensils.

The tracery of the east window, unlike all the other windows, is formed of fine-grained yellow sandstone and is a nineteenth-century insertion by a Dowager Lady Dunsany, adapted from a pattern similar to the east window at Killeen. The ancient sill can still be seen from the outside. There are three windows on the south and one on the north side. The west gable has a large window but the tracery is gone.

The church has three corner turrets and the strong north tower has a three-storied residence. There is a squint from the second floor of the sacristy looking down on the chancel.

The sedilium of three stalls recessed into the chancel south wall are original. According to the will of Christopher Plunkett, 1st Baron of Dunsany, he was "to be buried in the Chancel of Killeen". If the church in Dunsany was only nearing completion, possibly Christopher and Anne were re-interred in Dunsany.

The Plunkett Altar Tomb, in the north side chapel, carries the recumbent effigies of a knight wearing full armour, conical helmet, long sword at his left thigh, hands raised in prayer, with his feet resting on a sporting dog. The lady lies to his right, wearing a peaked headdress and long-sleeved long pleated gown, her feet resting on a cushion carved with two birds and a cat's head.

The tomb has four slabs, north, south, east and west, but all are now broken. The north slab has the following arms: Plunketts (bend and castle), Flemying (checguy), Castlemartin (three castles), Plunkett and Fitzgerald (bend and castle, saltire). The south slab has shields of Plunkett and Fitzgerald, a heart pierced by two swords and the instruments of the passion. The east slab has three niches with bishop in pontificals in the right niche, a long-robed figure in the middle one, and the left niche is broken away. The west slab has three floriated niches with the flagellation of our Lord in the centre and an angel with a censer on each side.

In the east wall is fixed a large black marble tablet bearing the following inscription:

Here lyeth the body of Sir Bryan O'Neill Bart.,
one of the Justices of the Kings's bench
in the reign of King James the 2nd
and died the 17th of October 1697,
and the Body of Dame Mary his wife,
Sister to the Lord Dunsany, and the
Body of Dame Mary O'Neill the second Sir Bryan's
Son who erected this tomb Anno Domini 1706.

At the other side of the east window is a slab of red granite in memory of Randal (1848-1883), son of Lord Dunsany, who died in Madeira.

The church was dismantled, presumably by Cromwell, but took on a temporary restoration when it was used as the location for the wedding scene in the film *Braveheart in 1994.*

Lady Mary Plunkett writes in 1902, that "my great uncle, Lord Louth, used to keep his hounds in the old church and you can still see where the windows were bricked up to prevent the hounds from jumping out".

The Plunkett Altar Tomb

DUNSANY FONT

In the chancel of the manorial church stands a fine ancient font. It stands 3 feet 6 inches high and has an octagonal head 26 inches across with basin and drain.

The carvings on the font are:

(1) Two angels supporting a shield with the instruments of the passion.
Below a pelican in piety, amidst foliage, as a type of Christ.

(2) St Peter with the keys and St Paul with the Sword. Below is fretwork-like groining (angular curve formed by crossing of two arches).

(3) St Andrew with his cross and St Thomas with a spear. Below are a hound and a hare with foliage.

(4) St Bartholomew with a knife and St James (the Minor) with a club. Below are trefoil-headed flutings.

(5) A saint with a long staff (perhaps St James the Major) and another saint with a halbert (perhaps St Matthias). Below plain fluting.

(6) Two saints. Below a pattern of fleurs-de-lis and trefoils.

(7) A saint and St Matthew with his bag. Below are birds and fleur-de-lis.

(8) The crucifixion between the Blessed Virgin and St John (the latter with a book). Below are interlaced leaves.

On the faces of the piers are:

(1)   Fretwork

(Two to five, angels bearing armorial shields)

(2)   The Crux Humanae Salvationis shown as a Latin cross with accompanying instruments.

(3)   The Arma Virginis, Our Lady's coat of arms, formed of a heart resting on or transfixed by two swords laid saltire-wise.

(4)   A saltire cross, the arms of Fitzgerald or FitzEustace.

(5)   A bend and tower, the Plunkett arms.

(6 & 7) Sprays of foliage

(8)   Flutings.

Isaac Butler, making his journey through Dunsany in (or a little after) 1740, places the font as near the west window; it now stands in the chancel.

Over the years the font has received considerable attention and, with the deterioration of the stone, the records left behind are valuable. There seems to be some conflict in identifying the arms on pier (4) as Fitzgerald (circa 1445) or FitzEustace (circa 1482). The general consensus of opinion is that the coat of arms belongs to the Fitzgerald family; Anne, of course, being the first wife of Christopher Plunkett who started the Dunsany Plunkett dynasty.

As can be seen from Thomas Westropp's drawings, in its prime this must have been an extremely beautiful apostle font. No trace of colouring has been found.

View of Font, Church of St. Nicholas, with details enlarged

DUNSANY WAYSIDE CROSS

Opposite the north-east Gothic entrance to Dunsany Castle stands a wayside cross. Standing on a circular stone block atop a square platform with four steps, there are two round basin holes in the base which may originally have been holy water fonts so that passers-by could bless themselves.

The shaft, which is 7 feet 8 inches high, 8 inches wide, and 5 inches thick, has a carving of the crucifixion near the top, above which is a winged ox, the symbol of St Luke.

The cross is thought to date from about 1600.

(Photograph: Paul Tierney)

HORACE CURSON PLUNKETT

Horace Curson Plunkett was born on 24th October, 1854, the sixth child of the 16th Baron of Dunsany, in his mother's ancestral home (Sherborne, Gloucestershire, England). Lady Dunsany died when Horace was four and subsequently the family returned to Dunsany Castle.

Many factors seem to have aroused and developed Horace's keen interest in agriculture. During his education in England he followed carefully the effects of the Industrial Revolution and noted the drainage of people from the land towards the industrialised cities.

In 1878, after his university years at Oxford, and having become interested in the co-operative movement, he opened the Co-operative Store in Dunsany, Co. Meath - his pilot store. However, it was in America that Horace's dreams and aspirations for Ireland developed. He suffered from tuberculosis and travelled to America for health reasons, where, during the years 1879-1889, he ranched in Wyoming, returning to Ireland only for the hunting season. It was here that Horace pondered on the severity of Ireland's social, domestic and agricultural problems. He was a man who used his family motto to the full. Festina Lente - working slowly, patiently and indomitably. While in a sanatorium in America, he became friendly with Dr J. H. Kellogg, who later with his brother, W. K., founded the now-famous cereal company of that name. (The Kellogg Foundation financed the I.C.A. headquarters at An Grianan, the sunny place, at Termonfechin, Co. Louth, which has become such an important centre for their activities.)

Horace worked hard for the betterment of Ireland's struggling farming community, giving freely of his time, energy and money when, due to ill health and his ascendancy background, he could easily have chosen to live a life of ease. Possibly, Gladstone's Land Act of 1881 (3 Fs: fair rent, fixture of tenure and free sale) indicated to him the direction in which the small farmers were beginning to move. Initially, this found expression in the formation of the Agricultural Co-operative Movement in Ireland. In this he was ably assisted by the Reverand Finlay, S.J., and George Russell, A.E. In 1889 the movement opened a co-operative store in Doneraile, Co. Cork and a creamery in Drumcollogher, Co. Limerick. The co-operative movement gained momentum despite heavy opposition. It is this aspect of his work that is best remembered, but his achievement in establishing the Department of Agriculture and Technical Instruction (DATI) is of equal, if not more importance.

In all his ventures Horace had a faithful friend in Elizabeth (Daisy) Fingall. In the book *Seventy Years Young*, the Countess describes herself as the "honeypot" coaxing people to become involved in Horace's plans and fundraising.[1]

Horace's idea for the Department of Agriculture was promoted through the Recess Committee, which he founded in 1896. Its objective was to discover how, without political change, Ireland could be provided with a Department of Agriculture.

Education, organisation and representation were to be the guiding principles. Horace states in his book, Ireland in the New Century: "Those who are familiar with the story of Ireland know how it came about that between two sections of the Irish people stands a great dividing wall, the foundations of which are racial, the stones political and the cement religious". Part of his intentions in founding a Department of Agriculture for Ireland was to unite Protestant and Catholic, unionist and nationalist, rich and poor, in the struggle to stabilise the ever-declining state of agriculture in the country.

Plunkett did not confine himself to Irish issues however. In 1895, while in America, he encountered Theodore Roosevelt, who became President shortly after the assassination of McKinley. Like Plunkett, he had spent some time ranching in Dakota and was very interested in rural development. He was fascinated by Plunkett's activities in Ireland, the co-operative movement, the Recess Committee and the work of D.A.T.I. "I wish you were an American and in the senate of my Cabinet," he wrote in 1906, "you take an interest in just the problems I regard as vital and you approach them in what seems to me to be the only sane and healthy way". He adopted Horace's slogan of "Better Farming, Better Business, Better Living" and said, "I'll megaphone it to the world". He

Elizabeth Fingall regales us with many interesting facts and trivia about Horace. (Apparently the only flower he ever liked was heliotrope; she also shares stories about his eccentric manservant, Reid, and the naming of his horses - Tripod, Biscay, Cyclops, Fitzgerald.) As Trevor West writes in the foreword to *Seventy Years Young*, "Lady Fingall was, of course, involved with most of his schemes. She acted as hostess at Plunkett's dinner-parties and as interior designer for Kilteragh, his house in Foxrock; she grew tobacco in her garden and cider apples in the orchard. 'Bottle the Boyne' was to be the slogan and, in 1910, inspired by AE, in conjunction with the poet Emily Lawless, (another Plunkett cousin), she became founder-member of the United Irish-women, which was a prototype for the Women's Institutes in Britain, and flourishes as the Irish Countrywomen's Association today. Lady Fingall's relationship lasted (probably unconsummated - he was an exceptionally fastidious man) without ever rupturing the friendship with his cousin, the Earl. He remained a bachelor for the sake of Lady Fingall and was unquestionably in love with her. However, Bernard Shaw was to remark years later, *'Yet I never felt convinced that he quite liked her'.*"

appointed a Commission on Country Life, and Plunkett together with Gifford Pinchot, a member of the U.S. cabinet, drafted the Commission's report. It recommended many of the themes advocated by Horace Plunkett: better rural schooling, better business and better living on the farms, etc. Its report remains a charter and major influence on rural philosophy in America.

On 1st August, 1896, a report was presented to the Lord Lieutenant of Ireland. The bill for the formation of the Department of Agriculture and Industry was proposed in April 1897 and rejected. The rejection gave the Committee more time to perfect their schemes. Many varied projects within the agricultural sphere were undertaken in and around Dunsany: goatherds, tobacco crops and numerous orchards appeared in what had been prime paddocks! In 1899, Gerald Balfour re-introduced the revised bill and this was passed. The Department of Agriculture and Technical Instruction at last was a reality and Horace Plunkett was, subsequently, appointed vice president. Now the responsibilities for this whole area were firmly based in Ireland.

In 1901, Horace submitted a memorandum on education for Ireland on behalf of the Department. This document outlined the plan to incorporate agricultural education and thus encourage farmers' sons to attend school until they were older.

In 1908, Horace published his essay "Noblisse Oblige", addressed to the despondent gentry of Ireland. He encourages them to remain on their estates, depleted by the Wyndham Land Purchase Act of 1903 (the compulsory purchase of land by tenants). He calls on them, with their superior education and knowledge, to teach small farmers and assist them on the

road to prosperity.
By 1914 there were 1023 co-operative societies in Ireland; because of its non-political stance the movement attracted a lot of people.

Horace, despite being an Unionist M.P., headed many successful ventures such as the I.A.O.S. (Irish Agricultural Organisation Society), the C.D.B.(Congested Districts Board), United Irish Women (the forerunner of the I.C.A.) and many others, against a background of fierce political activity and unrest. He won many followers, not by his ability to make speeches, but by a total sincerity which led him to plough his own fortune into his various undertakings.

Another facet of Plunkett's work was the establishment of the so-called "Land Banks". These were designed to provide loans for farmers and small businesses at a low rate of interest, which in the course of time, led to the formation of the modern credit union movement.

On the other hand, he had many disappointments, including election defeat, his enforced resignations from the D.A.T.I. and the disastrous reception of his book *Ireland in the New Century*.[2]

---

[2]It was rejected by the Church and the Nationalists. One wrote, "Horace has demonstrated his unfitness for his position by wantonly and deliberately insulting the character and religion of the great majority of the Irish people, to whom he appeals for co-operation". However, in an epilogue later written by The Honorable Horace Plunkett, he states that "the purpose was to concentrate thought upon certain social and economic problems hitherto neglected in Ireland, to expound a practical programme of national development"; clearly his ideas were misunderstood.

In 1922, because of his seat in the Senate and regardless of the fact that he had petitioned for leniency in the sentences of the 1916 rebels, Horace's house was mined and burned by the IRA. Frustrated and heartbroken, he retired to England. Kilteragh, apart from being the house he loved, was an experimental farm where endless new projects to improve Irish agriculture were being tested. Here he had entertained many of Ireland's distinguished thinkers - Jack B. Yeats, Lady Gregory, Michael Collins, Douglas Hyde and George Bernard Shaw and many more. His guest book survived the fire and is presently in Trinity College.

Many of the major contributions that Horace Plunkett made to agricultural life in the first half of the last century have really only been acknowledged and appreciated in the latter half. He contributed so much to the economic life of this country and his dedication can be summed up in one of his farewell remarks before leaving Ireland: "what wouldn't a man do for a country like this?"[3]

Horace died at 7:15p.m the evening of 26th March, 1932.

His reputation continues to grow. At the end of 1999, Horace Plunkett was voted by the *Irish Farmers Monthly* 'Farm Person of the Century'.

[3]However, much of the bitterness and sadness that this hard-working Protestant gentleman must have felt departing to England would justify the rather arrogant speech that Yeats (himself an Anglo-Irishman) made a few years later when he deviated to speak in defense of the ascendancy:

"We are no petty people, we are of the great stocks of Europe, we are the people of Grattan, and we are the people of Swift, the people of Emmett, the people of Parnell. We have created most of the modern literature of this country. We have created the best of its political intelligence".

Sir Horace Plunkett   *C.1909*

ST OLIVER'S FAMILY TREE

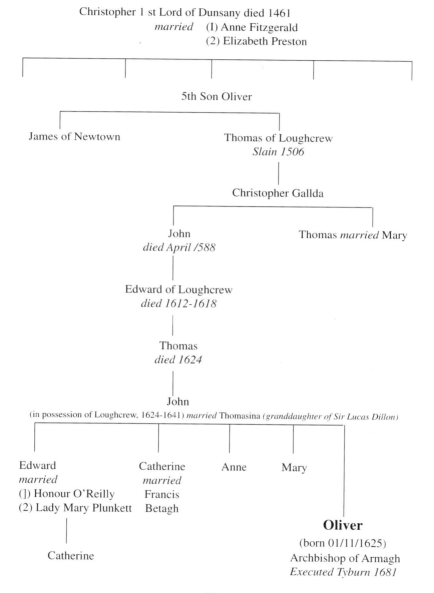

Christopher 1 st Lord of Dunsany died 1461
married (I) Anne Fitzgerald
(2) Elizabeth Preston

5th Son Oliver

James of Newtown

Thomas of Loughcrew
Slain 1506

Christopher Gallda

John
died April /588

Thomas *married* Mary

Edward of Loughcrew
died 1612-1618

Thomas
died 1624

John
(in possession of Loughcrew, 1624-1641) *married* Thomasina *(granddaughter of Sir Lucas Dillon)*

Edward
married
(]) Honour O'Reilly
(2) Lady Mary Plunkett

Catherine
married
Francis
Betagh

Anne

Mary

Catherine

Oliver
(born 01/11/1625)
Archbishop of Armagh
Executed Tyburn 1681

ST OLIVER PLUNKETT

St Oliver does not refer to his personal life, or the names of his immediate family or ancestors, in the extensive collection of his correspondence in ecclesiastical archives. The adjacent family tree outlines as near as possible the saint's lineage. One fact that is certain is that the date of his birth was 1st November, 1625. This fact came to light when a twin horoscope, now in the Bodleian Library, Oxford, was discovered referring to John Milton (the poet) and Oliver Plunkett.

St Oliver Plunkett's mother had an aunt, Genet Dillon, who had married Christopher Plunkett, 9th Baron of Killeen, and these were the parents of his second cousin, Patrick Plunkett. Patrick entered the Cistercian Order and served in many locations, becoming Bishop of Ardagh in 1647 and Bishop of Meath in 1669. It is this cousin who is thought to have influenced Oliver Plunkett as a boy in pursuing a religious life and, in consequence, it is presumed that he would have been on familiar territory visiting the castles of Dunsany and Killeen.

On 19th October, 1668, Dr Patrick Plunkett wrote as follows to his relative Dr Oliver Plunkett, who was then an agent of the Irish Church in Rome:

"As regards your relatives, the Earls of Fingall and Roscommon have re-acquired their lands and property, which were in the hands of Cromwell's Officers, and to the great delight of all friends, the Castle of Killeen has been restored to Lord Fingall. The Baron of Dunsany having not recovered any of his estates is reduced to great poverty; but the Baron of Louth has obtained a partial restitution of what he lost. Mr. Nicholas Plunkett of

Dunsaile has got back all his former possessions. The other Plunketts, of Tatrath, Balrath and Preston, have not yet got back their castles which are still in the hands of the Cromwellians and Londoners, having been purchased by them from the Parliament in the time of the rebellion."

Loughcrew, near Oldcastle, Co. Meath, the home of St Oliver Plunkett's family, was forfeited at the time of Oliver Cromwell's invasion of Ireland and has remained in the possession of the Napier family who acquired it.[1]

In 1647, Oliver had gone to Rome and lived there for twenty-two years as a clerical student and, later, professor of theology. He was ordained on 1st January, 1654, by Bishop MacGeoghan, at a very private ceremony in the Propaganda College, although he was a student of the Irish College. Oliver returned to Ireland in 1670 as Archbishop of Armagh and Primate. In December 1673, the campaign of persecution resumed and the Bishop opted to be a fugitive in various places of refuge rather than abandon his flock.

Oliver was arrested on 6th December, 1679, and remained in close confinement in Dublin Castle. In July, 1680, there was an abortive trial in Dundalk, and he was transferred to Newgate Prison in October of that year. In May 1681, Oliver Plunkett was arraigned and given only five weeks to bring witnesses from Ireland. On 8th June, six days before their arrival, he was put on trial and found guilty on perjured evidence, the charge being high treason. The sentence was death, to be hanged, drawn and quartered.

---

[1]An annual open-air Mass is held in the grounds of the estate, with the old manorial church as a backdrop for the ceremony, which coincides with his Feast Day.

Back in his cell in Newgate, a tremendous peace and serenity took possession of the Archbishop's soul as he prepared for death. A letter dated 22nd June, reached Rome and its recipient, young Father Michael Plunkett at the Irish College, handed it over to Propaganda. He writes: "sentence of death was passed against me on the 15th but it has not terrified nor caused me to lose even a quarter of an hour of sleep. I am as innocent of all treason as the child born yesterday......[2]"

Dr Plunkett had the privilege of offering Mass in his cell early in the morning before his captors came for him. At Tyburn he read the speech which he had prepared, reaffirming his innocence and forgiving his accusers, and then calmly offered

[2]The complete letter reads: "sentence of death was passed against me on the 15th but it has not terrified nor caused me to lose even a quarter of an hour of sleep. I am as innocent of all treason as the child born yesterdayAs for my character (priestly and episcopal), profession (of the Catholic faith) and function (as Archbishop of Armagh), I did own it publicly, and that being also a motive of my death I die most willingly. And as the first amongst the Irish, with God's grace I shall give others the good example not to fear death. But how am I, a poor creature, so stout-hearted, seeing that my Redeemer began to be afraid and to be sad, and that drops of his blood trickled down upon the ground? I have considered that Christ by his fears and sufferings merited for me to be without fear... I do forgive all who had a hand directly or indirectly in my death and in my innocent blood... My accusers swore that I had 7,000 men in Ireland to promote the Catholic cause, and that I had the harbour of Carlingford ready to bring in the French - such romances as would not be believed by any jury in Ireland... I expect daily to be brought to the place of my execution where my bowels are to be cut out and burned before my face, and then my head to be cut off, etc., which death I embrace willingly: I desire to be dissolved and to be with Christ. I salute all my friends over there as if I had named them and I recommend myself to their prayers. None of them ought to be grieved for my death, being as innocent as what is laid to my charge as a child unborn, as to the matter of treason. As for my religion and character, 'tis glorious for all my friends that I should die for it."

himself to the executioners. On his dying lips where the words of his dying Saviour:"Into your hands, O Lord, I commend my spirit". This happened on 1st July 1681, reign of Charles II. He was the last person to be executed at Tyburn for the Catholic faith.

St Oliver Plunkett's portrait has always had a special location in Dunsany Castle where he is regarded, rightfully, as a descendant of the original family. Important relics remain with the family: his episcopal ring, the crook of his travelling crosier and his watch.

He was beatified on 23rd May, 1920 and canonised on 12th October, 1975 by Pope Paul VI. St Oliver Plunkett was the first Irish saint in almost 700 years. Many of the Plunkett family attended this wonderful celebration of his life and death, including Edward Plunkett and Randall, 19th Lord Dunsany. Apart from the solemn ceremonies and the privilege of a papal audience, this unique occasion provided the opportunity for a family reunion.

St. Oliver Plunkett's episcopal ring and watch
(Drawing by Michéal O'Brien)

Loughcrew c.1655

(Paul Tierney)

CORBALLY CASTLE

Corbally Castle is located in the townland of Corballis, Dunsany. Nothing now remains but the earthworks; the stones from the tower castle may have been recycled into adjacent walls and piers.

The only record of the castle is in the charter of James I, restoring the castles of Dunsany and Corbally to Lord Dunsany. It would appear that originally the castle belonged to Cusack of Belpere and there are several references in documents relating to this family. The castle is shown on the Down Survey map. The table below from the Civil Survey, 1654, would seem to indicate that there was a village at Corballis.

Proprietors in 1640 & their Qualifications	**The Parish of Donsany**		
	The said Parish is bounded on the east with Killeene Parish, on ye west with Killmessan Parrish, on the south with Knockmarke Parish, And on ye north with Taragh Parish		
Patrick Ld Baron of Donsany Irish Papist	In the said Parish are these ensueing Townes & Villages Donsany & Corballis		
	Donsany & Corballis One plowland	Acres 240	Arable 200 Mead 10 Pasture 30
	The said towne of Donsany and Corballis Being the whole Parish is bounded as aforesaid		

At the time of the beautification of Blessed Margaret Bermingham (Ball), it was speculated that this could be the Corballis in Co. Meath where she had spent her youth. Members of the Bermingham family had married into the Dunsany family.

TRIM CASTLE

Trim castle, built in three phases between 1175 and 1205, has a long and colourful history, acting as a stronghold and garrison for Normans, Royalists and Cromwellians. With the restoration of Charles II the necessity for a large garrison lessened. By 1663, the castle had become extremely dilapidated and suffered the degradation of being vandalised. Adam Loftus, custodian, was appointed that year. Dean Butler records that the castle and its lands passed on 26th June, 1667, from Adam Loftus of Rathfarnham, Co. Dublin, to Sir James Shean for a sum of £7,200.

In the aftermath of the Williamite confiscation, ownership passed to the Wellesley family of Dangan. In 1822, Arthur Wellesley, Duke of Wellington, decided to sell up the family estate and leave Ireland. The auction catalogue still survives in the National Library of Ireland. Lot 53 is described as: The ancient grand structure, King John's Castle, one of the superb ruins of the Kingdom, situated on the banks of the River Boyne. The principal part surrounded by the old walls, the castle yard, etc.". Colonel Leslie of Glaslough, Co. Monaghan, was the purchaser, but his son sold it again in 1859. The new owners were the Plunkett family of Dunsany whose castle home had also been built by Hugh de Lacy.

Some years after the Plunkett family's acquisition of Trim Castle, John, the 17th Lord Dunsany, refused to vest Trim Castle in the Board of National Monuments.[1]

Trim Castle passed back to the State in 1993.

[1]He expressed himself quite explicitly in a letter dated 7th September, 1893. He said he was "no more disposed than my father was to let Trim Castle pass into the hands of any Board", and that his father would have carried out more repairs were it not for the attempts made "to alienate from owners all that gives them pride and pleasure and interest in maintaining intact such objects of interest. I have during my four years tenure of my Irish property, completely restored the tumbling ruin of the old Church at Dunsany, and, by preventing (by locks, gates, etc.) Trim Castle being, as it had almost become, public property (and even a public quarry) put a stop to the gradual demolition of the building. All respectable people are free to visit it, I have had many parties there, but I intend to keep it as one of the sources of pleasure that I can offer my guests. If it is dangerous to the public, I will close it to the public, but I have taken many ladies over it all and intend to make it all more accessible and perfectly safe, witness the old ruin at Dunsany. I hope this will be understood to be final as far as it is the expression of my intention to keep my own property in my own hands".

EXTENDED PLUNKETT FAMILY

From the time of their arrival in Ireland the Plunkett family has prospered. Their ability to succeed in various professions has often caused comment.

King Edward VII said to Elizabeth Plunkett, Countess of Fingall at Dublin Castle:"I never seem to get away from Plunketts in this country. There is Lord Plunkett, Sir Horace Plunkett, Bishop Plunkett, Colonel Plunkett, Count Plunkett and that horrid little boy of yours treading on the Queen's train"! (Young Oliver Plunkett, the last Earl of Fingall.)

Branches of the family are now located in many parts of the world. St Oliver's canonisation gave the clan an opportunity for an informal reunion. Technology and the introduction of web sites have given the Plunketts a new medium for dialogue.

THE

POOR MAN'S GUARDIAN,
A Weekly Paper
FOR THE PEOPLE.

PUBLISHED IN DEFIANCE OF " LAW," TO TRY THE POWER
OF " RIGHT " AGAINST " MIGHT."

" IT IS THE CAUSE; IT IS THE CAUSE."

No. 39.] | *Saturday, March 10, 1832.* | [Price 1*d*.

THE NOBLE ARMY OF PLUNKETS!!!
A Formidable Array.

	£		
Lord Plunket's salary as Chancellor	£8,000	0	0
The Hon. and Rev. Thomas Plunket, as Dean of Down, and with other church income	3,000	0	0
The Hon. David Plunket, as Prothonotary of the Court of Common Pleas	1,500	0	0
Said Hon. David, as Examiner in Common Pleas	600	0	0
Four offices in the said Court, in the gift of said Hon. David, at £500 each per annum	2,000	0	0
One of £300 (cum aliis)	300	0	0
The Hon. John Plunket, as Commissioner of Inquiry	1,300	0	0
The Hon. John, as Assistant Barrister of Co. Meath..	700	0	0
Said Hon. John, as Crown Counsel on Munster Circuit	500	0	0
Aforesaid Hon. John, as Counsel to the Police	400	0	0
The Hon. and Rev. William Plunket, as VICAR of BRAY	700	0	0
The Honourable Patrick Plunket, as Purse Bearer to the Chancellor	500	0	0
The Honourable Patrick, as Secretary of Bankrupts	600	0	0
The Honourable Patrick, as Crown Counsel on the Leinster Circuit	400	0	0
Honourable Patrick Plunket, as Counsel to Chief Remembrancer	350	0	0
The Honourable Robert Plunket, by a Church preferment in England presented by Lord Goderich, in 1829	1,300	0	0
William James M'Causland, Esq., Law Agent for Commissioners of Donations and Charitable Bequests and Brother-in-law of Lord Plunket	600	0	0
Said Wm. James M'Causland, Brother-in-Law, as aforesaid, Solicitor for Minors and Lunatics	1,400	0	0
Said Mr. James M'Causland, as Law Agent to Commissioners of Education	400	0	0
Said William James, as Solicitor to the Board of Erasmus Smith	1,200	0	0
Said William James's Son, Richard B. M'Causland, Nephew to Lord Plunket, Joint Secretary of the Lord Chancellor	1,500	0	0
Said William James's Brother, the Rev. Mr. M'Causland, Church Income through the influence of Lord Plunket	1,200	0	0
Sum Total of the Money drained annually by the Reforming Plunket family out of the Public Purse	28,450	0	0

SOURCES

Barony Maps of Down Survey, 1657

Blessed Oliver Plunkett Historical Studies   by Fr. Paul Walsh, 1937

Burke's Landed Gentry of Ireland   Sir Bernard Burke 1958

Carew Manuscripts on the Temporal   Lambeth Palace
Nobility & Will of Sir Christopher   Library, London
Plunkett of Dunsany

Civil Survey, 1654 - 1656   Robert Simington

Debrett's Peerage & Baronetage

Dunsany 1894 - 1994   D.Lynch, J.Donohue & M.Smith

Notes on Dunsany   by Beryl F. E Moore, M.B,

Dunsany Castle, Co. Meath   by John Cornforth
Country Life, May 27th, 1971

History of Killeen Castle   Mary-Rose Carty, 1991

Historic Irish Mansions   by James Fleming
The Weekly Irish Times
September 11th, 1937

Horace Plunkett - Co-Operation   by Trevor West, 1986
and Politics - An Irish Biography

Horace Plunkett - An Anglo-American   by Margaret Digby, 1949
Irishman

Guide to the Archives of the Office   The Stationery Office
of Public Works - 1994

Ireland in the New Century   by Horace Plunkett, 1904

Irish Farmers Monthly   December, 1999
Late Medieval Ireland, 1370-1541   by Art Gosgrove

Lord Dunsany: A Biography   by Mark Amory, 1972

Lord Dunsany: King of Dreams   by Hazel Littlefield, 1959

Medieval Fonts of Meath   by Helen M. Roe, 1968

National Library of Ireland

Nobilisse Oblige	by Horace Plunkett, 1908
Notes on Rawlinson B 512	Bodleian Library, Oxford
Ordinance Survey Office, Dublin	
Origin of Irish Families	by Edward MacLysaght
The Cusacks of Killeen, Co. Meath Riocht na Midhe - 1980|81	by Pearse Cusack, O. Cist.
Seventy Years Young Re-published, April 1991, Lilliput Press in association with Carty|Lynch	Memories of Elizabeth, Countess of Fingall
Skryne and the Early Normans 1994	by Elizabeth Hickey
The Buildings of Ireland, Volume: North Leinster	C. Casey & A. Rowan Penguin Books 1993
The Complete Peerage Volume IV	by G.E.C.
The Cusack Family of Meath & Dublin (The Irish Genealogist) Parts IV, V & VI	by Hubert Gallwey
The Journal of the Royal Society *of Antiquaries of Ireland* - 1894 The Church of Dunsany, Co. Meath	by Thomas J. Westropp, M.A., Fellow
The Kin of Blessed Oliver Catholic Bulletin, December, 1935	by Fr Paul Brady
The Letters of Saint Oliver Plunkett 1979	edited by Monsignor J. Hanley
The Poor Man's Guardian	Editorial March 10, 1832
Trim Castle Re-published 1978 Meath Archaelogical Society	by Richard Butler
View of the Legal Institutions, *Honorary Hereditary Offices and* *Feudal Baronies Established in the* *Reign of Henry II, 1830*	by William Lynch
With Plunkett In Ireland 1983	by R. A. Anderson

ACKNOWLEDGEMENTS

Lord & Lady Dunsany

Jim & Sean Dungan

Sean Flynn

Anne Gray

Monsignor John Hanley

Paul Tierney

Ms Marsha Swan (Proof Reader)

Staff of: Bodleian Library, Oxford

Staff of: Lambeth Palace Library, London

Staff of: Meath County Library

Staff of: National Library of Ireland

Wife and family of Malachy Lynch

Husband and family of Mary-Rose Carty